THE AGE OF ILLUSION

THE AGE OF
ILLUSION

ART AND POLITICS
IN FRANCE
1918-1940

DOUGLAS AND MADELEINE JOHNSON

284 illustrations

THAMES AND HUDSON

This book, which is essentially about Paris, is dedicated to two friends who live there, Sylvie and Eric Boissonnas.

Frontispiece: The Eiffel Tower, drawing by Robert Delaunay.

Designed by Ruth Rosenberg

Picture research by Georgina Bruckner

© 1987 Thames and Hudson Ltd

Printed and bound in Japan by Dai Nippon.

CONTENTS

Poster for Renoir's masterpiece, *La Grande Illusion* (1937), set in a prison camp in the 1914–18 War.

When we talk of 'la Belle Epoque', we are usually referring to the 'good old days' before 1914. The Third Republic had been born in 1870, out of the defeat of France by Prussia; it had suffered the blood-bath of the Commune in Paris, when Frenchmen had shot Frenchmen in what could be called the civil war of 1871; it had been threatened with other civil wars, as when General Boulanger had seemed to be on the verge of establishing a new Bonapartism in the 1880s, or when Frenchmen could not agree whether or not a certain Captain Dreyfus had been rightly convicted of treason in the 1890s. But the Third Republic had settled down. It appeared that France was a calm country governed by overwrought politicians. A powerful bourgeoisie, linked with banks and finance; a lesser bourgeoisie, associated with small enterprises; a multitude of officials; and an old-fashioned peasantry; all seemed to be united. They agreed about order, about law, about patriotism. They were confident in their strength and in their superiority over socialists, anarchists and strike organizers. They were able to put up with the innovations which Impressionists and post-Impressionists brought to art, they could tolerate the experiments in music by Claude Debussy or Erik Satie, and they could accommodate themselves to the new poetry of a Rimbaud or of an Apollinaire. 'Famille, je vous haïs', Gide could cry in *Les Nourritures terrestres* (1897), but the French family was solid, based upon male supremacy, and a devotion either to the Catholic Church or to the Republic or to both. These years have also been described as 'the banquet years'. Paris was the world centre of culture, of fashion, of amusement.

But could the Belle Epoque survive the 1914 war? Could France after 1914 ever know another Belle Epoque? Those who believed that the war would be short and the victory easy for the French and their Russian and British allies were soon disillusioned. The war became a long-drawn-out agony, with ten departments of northern France occupied by the Germans. Every plan to break the military deadlock failed. There was bitterness, war-weariness and disillusionment, as the attrition continued and the casualties mounted. By November 1918, 1.4 million French citizens had been killed.

And no one expected that November 1918 would be the month in which an armistice would be signed. Russia had dropped out of the war, and even though American troops were pouring into France they were not expected to be a match for the apparently inexhaustible German army. In the summer of 1918 the Germans had forced their way across the Marne and were within sixty kilometres of Paris, which they were bombarding with their huge cannon, the Big Bertha. But by July the Allied armies under Foch were able to launch an effective series of offensives. Germany's position on other fronts, in the Balkans, in Syria, in Italy, deteriorated. Her allies fell away. By the end of September the German High Command agreed that an armistice should be sought.

The images which illustrate the events that followed are significant. In a railway carriage in the forest of Rethondes near to Compiègne, the French generals Foch and Weygand dictated the armistice terms, while a much less exalted British delegation assisted. The resolute Clemenceau, Prime Minister since 1917 and hailed as Père la Victoire, went to Strasbourg in Alsace and celebrated the return to France of that province and Lorraine, which had been annexed to Germany in 1870. The peace conference was held in Paris and the peace treaty was signed in the Hall of Mirrors in the Palace of Versailles on 28 June 1919. On the anniversary of the fall of the Bastille, on 14 July of that year, the traditional military review became a victory parade, above all a celebration of the heroism of the French army and of its leader Henri Philippe Pétain, the man who had held the Germans at the battle of Verdun in 1916 and who had preserved the morale of the troops in the difficult years of 1917 and 1918. On that day no one could doubt: France was the greatest power on the continent. It seemed that a new sort of Belle Epoque was about to begin.

The story of France between the two world wars can almost be told in terms of crowd scenes in Paris: from the celebrations of 1918 and 1919, through the political demonstrations and processions of the 1920s and the 1930s, down to the greatest crowd movement of all, the *exode* of 1940, when the roads of France became an endless succession of refugees fleeing from the advancing German armies and Paris became a deserted city.

But even when the crowd scenes were those of celebration, French politics were such that there were always complications. The President of the Republic, Poincaré, himself a Lorrainer who had particularly celebrated the recovery of this lost province, was coming to the end of his term. The most famous French statesman by the end of 1919 was Clemenceau. But within the narrow world of French politics his authoritarianism, his putting down of strikes and his anti-clericalism had earned him many enemies. So the President of the Assembly, the somewhat colourless Paul Deschanel, was elected in his stead. This proved to be an unhappy choice. On 11 November 1920 a great ceremony was to take place, inaugurating the tomb of the Unknown Soldier at the Arc de Triomphe. Some time before this Deschanel had shown unmistakable signs of mental instability. He could not be trusted to preside at this ceremony. Therefore he had to be removed and the then Prime Minister Alexandre Millerand took his place. Solemnity was etched by the ridiculous. Nothing was going to be easy.

Public life in France was to be dominated by three questions. The first was that of the stagnation of the French population. Not only had many Frenchmen been killed during the four years of fighting, more than a million had been permanently disabled, there had been an increase in civilian deaths, and the birth-rate had been unusually low. Adding the deaths to the births which had not taken place, the loss during the war came to some 3 million. And this demographic haemorrhage was inflicted upon a society which, even prior to 1914, had experienced a relative decline of its population, since the bourgeoisie, preoccupied by the prosperity of their children, had voluntarily restricted births, while the level of infantile mortality had remained high.

There were several consequences. Those French women who, before the war, had been active in working for the right to vote and for changes in the law which always favoured males, were told in no uncertain manner that their duty to France was to raise families rather than to agitate politically. The Catholic Church felt that it was acting in the interests of the nation as a whole when it urged its members to produce children. Those concerned with the defence of France believed that a special effort had to be made to protect France against a traditional enemy which had a young and buoyant population. Some believed that because the French were becoming scarcer ('le Français se fait rare', as Giraudoux put it) there was everything to be gained by allowing foreign workers to immigrate (originally Spaniards, Italians and Poles), and this created problems which became acute in the 1930s when unemployment began to rise.

The second question was that of finance. Whether it was because a harsh taxation policy would have been unbearable in a country undergoing the agonies of the war, or whether, as cynics put it, because the bourgeoisie was ready to give its sons to France but not its gold, the war had been financed by a series of expensive loans. After the war the devastated areas of the country, whether cities, mines, industrial areas or farmlands, had to be reconstructed, and this was also paid for by loans. The myth grew that everything would be paid for by the Germans who had been named in the peace treaty as guilty of having caused the war. But by the mid-1920s it was clear that this would not happen. There was a loss of confidence in the franc, its value in the international money market dropped, there was a flight of capital away from France. Successive governments found themselves financially embarrassed and unable to raise loans. Not until 1926 was the panic stopped by Poincaré, who returned to government as Premier, devalued the franc and announced measures which restored confidence.

Among the consequences of this financial instability was a neurosis about the franc. There was a clinging to the Poincaré franc (which was aligned to gold from 1928) as if the stability of the currency was the only important thing about the country's economy.

The third great question was that of France's relations with the other European powers and with the world beyond Europe. France had been on the winning side of the war, but even the most nationalistic of Frenchmen were forced to recognize the vital importance of having had Russia, Britain, Italy and the United States as allies. Therefore France had to have security against Germany. During the peace negotiations the French delegation had demanded that Germany be dismembered or subjected to permanent military occupation. This was not accepted by France's allies and instead France was offered American and British treaties guaranteeing her security. But both offers became void in 1920 when the United States Senate refused to ratify the treaty.

The result was that every French statesman tried to find a system which would give his country security. In 1923 French (and Belgian) troops occupied the Ruhr in order to enforce German payments of reparations, but this did not succeed and had to be abandoned the following year. In 1924 the newly elected Premier, Edouard Herriot, tried to organize French security within the League of Nations system, but this did not work. A specialist of foreign affairs, Aristide Briand, known as 'the pilgrim of peace', was one of the creators in 1926 of the Locarno Pact, which sought to guarantee the frontiers with the agreement of Germany. But the French were still not confident. Although in 1919 France had appeared to be the most powerful state on the continent, in terms of international diplomacy France was seen to be a more dependent power than many of the French were prepared to accept. Yet there seemed to be little that they could do about it.

The political system which had to respond to these three questions was essentially that which had been introduced after the Franco-Prussian war. France was a parliamentary democracy with two elected houses: the Senate and the Chamber of Deputies. The two houses together elected the President of the Republic, the head of state, who served for seven years but who became a ceremonial rather than an effective figure. Virtually all power lay with the Deputies. Their ability to make and unmake governments was all the greater because their Chamber was in practice immune from dissolution, and their disposition to do so was all the more probable because of the political confusions that existed among them. They were divided into three main sections (though there were several groups within each section): the Right, which existed under various labels; the Centre, which was frequently dominated by the Radicals; and the Left, which was Socialist, although in December 1920 this party split and the new Communist party emerged.

A few months after the signature of the Treaty of Versailles, in November 1919, there was a general election. For the first time since the earliest days of the Third Republic in 1871, it was the political right which was elected. So many of the deputies had served in the army and had worn uniform that the Assembly was known as 'la Chambre bleu horizon'. The election results were largely due to a change in the method of election, which was designed to reduce the parliamentary power of the Socialists.

The weaknesses of this political system were self evident. The President of the Republic, Millerand, who had succeeded the unfortunate Deschanel, talked about strengthening Presidential powers. But this caused alarm, since it seemed to threaten what many believed to be the sovereign rights of the National Assembly. In the elections of 1924, the Socialists who had remained within the old party ('la vieille maison', led by Léon Blum) collaborated with the Radicals of the centre, forming the so-called Cartel des Gauches and gaining the majority in the Assembly. Millerand was obliged to resign and the Radical leader, Edouard Herriot, formed a government. But further weaknesses in the system soon became apparent. The Socialists, although they were part of the Cartel for electoral purposes, refused to be members of the government. While the Assembly was dominated by the Cartel des Gauches, the Senate remained far more to the right and was able to thwart the government. Above all, the victory of the left had alarmed the banks and financial circles. In the spring of 1925 Herriot was defeated in the Senate and resigned. But within a year he was a member of the government led by Poincaré, which was orientated towards the right.

It was characteristic of the Radicals that although claiming oratorically to be on the left, especially at election times, they invariably ended up by collaborating with parties which were to the right of them. They were republicans, in the sense that they believed in the tradition of the Republic that had been established by the Revolution – the centralized, parliamentary and anti-clerical state. But they were also individualists, believing in the rights of the small property owner and suspicious of a state which would increase taxation and redistribute wealth. As a result they contributed to the instability of the system.

There were political traditions in France other than those that were parliamentary. There was the Bonapartist tradition of strong government. There were also protest groups, operating outside the system and determined to change it, if necessary by unconstitutional methods. When, after the elections of 1932, a series of unstable governments had to face up to the problems caused by the great international depression, there were those who believed in a fundamental reform of French institutions. Various organizations began to bring increasing violence into French political life. The Action Française, for example, which had been founded at the time of the Dreyfus affair, and which was dominated by the philosopher Charles Maurras and the journalist Léon Daudet, believed in the traditional values of pre-Revolutionary France, as represented by the monarchy, the Church, the local notabilities and the army. Within it was an activist group, the Camelots du Roi, and alongside it was formed an organization for ex-service men, the Croix-de-Feu. There were other right-wing groups, such as the Francistes, the Jeunesses Patriotes, and Solidarité Française, but none of them had the philosophical refinements of Maurras, and they were more concerned with immediate issues, such as denouncing the weak incompetence of successive governments and striving to achieve economic self-sufficiency for France. These movements, which were known collectively as the Leagues, blamed Communists and Socialists, Freemasons and pacifists, foreigners and Jews, for the country's misfortunes.

The opportunity for the Leagues appeared to come with revelations about government corruption. The most important of these concerned a swindler known as Stavisky. It was in 1933 that his exploits became widely known, and it appeared that he had been in trouble for many years but had escaped justice through influential friends in the judiciary, the police, parliament and, it was said, the government. Among the influential friends, whose support he had supposedly purchased, were many prominent Radical politicians. The scandal became sensational when in January 1934 Stavisky was found shot dead. The Leagues, and others, organized demonstrations in the streets, claiming that Stavisky had been murdered in order to prevent him from revealing the extent of government complicity in his crookedness.

It was on 6 February 1934 that a demonstration took place in Paris which turned into a lengthy and bloody riot in which many people were killed. The demonstrators tried to break into the National Assembly building (the Palais Bourbon) and were only just prevented. On the next day the government, which had the full support of the Assembly at this moment of crisis, resigned. It was the first government since 1848 to be overturned by a riot in the streets of Paris, and this seemed ominous. The outgoing Prime Minister, Edouard Daladier, a Radical who had not been involved in the Stavisky scandals, was frightened of further violence, and in order to reassure the country, the President (by this time Albert Lebrun) called on a former President of the Republic, Gaston Doumergue, to leave his retirement and return to power. It is a French political tradition to turn to well-known figures of the past when the country is in danger.

But the left was not reassured. They claimed to scent the danger of dictatorship and came together in counter-demonstrations and protest strikes. While this was a grass-roots reaction it was some time before the leaders of the Communist, Socialist and Radical parties were able to agree, and to work in an electoral alliance for the formation of a Popular Front government. Their victory in the spring of 1936 was largely due to this change of electoral tactics. The Popular Front parties gained a clear parliamentary majority, although they had only increased their share of the national vote by 1.5 percent and did not have a majority of those voting.

But a new era seemed to have dawned. Although the Communists refused to take part in the government, which was sinister, hopes ran high. The popular will had been demonstrated. A new man, Léon Blum, was in charge. Men of principle, who were bound to a programme which aimed at peace, liberty and social progress, had replaced the opportunistic politicians of the past and overthrown the menace of the Leagues. The enthusiasm of the crowds which had paraded in the streets and demonstrated their unity seemed to be matched by this great electoral victory.

This intense political life was centred in Paris. Although many prominent politicians had their fiefs in the provinces, and based their power on an assiduous cultivation of their local supporters, their activity was always Parisian. Deputies received a salary, and as professionals it was to the seat of power that they flocked. And this was another reason why Paris became yet more important in

France. Already the centre of the railway network, of banking, of the bureaucratic hierarchy, and of intellectual and social fashion, Paris between the wars became the hub of French life even more than it had been before 1914. The allegation was made that there was Paris; and that outside there was a desert which was the rest of France.

The growth of Paris was remarkable. In 1851 its population was about 1 million, that is to say some 3 percent of the country's total population. Sixty years later it contained 10 percent of the total population. In 1931 this rose to 14 percent, and this in a country which, if one counts a population of some 5,000 as forming a town, still had more than half of its population living outside towns. But this Paris of more than 2½ million people was only the heart of a shapeless agglomeration which, by 1936, contained more than 6 million inhabitants. The suburbs, where houses and factories stood in close, and sometimes grimy, proximity, had started to develop from the end of the nineteenth century; the interminable rows of small, detached houses came later and were mainly a phenomenon of the 1920s. Of the global increase of the total French population which took place between 1831 and 1936, well over half, 5 million out of 9 million, were absorbed by Paris and its suburbs (the three departments of the capital being the Seine, Seine-et-Oise, and Seine-et-Marne).

This is all the more emphatic a happening because it was taking place in a country which was suffering a general decline in population numbers. Within such a framework the growth of Paris was a unique phenomenon. To some extent it has to be explained by the war itself. Although Paris experienced Zeppelin raids and in 1918 was shelled by a German giant gun, and although Parisians were only too conscious of the unceasing transport of troops and wounded through their railway stations and of the high cost of living, Paris became something of a boom town during the war. The workforce increased as munition factories and other metallurgical enterprises were created in such places as Ivry, Choisy and Vitry; the Americans built the aerodrome at Orly, and the British and Americans opened up the railway station of Brétigny-sur-Orge as a vast depot for stores. Industries from the German-occupied departments of the north moved to Paris and the extension of many governmental activities meant that there was an increased demand for personnel coming from the ministries.

After the war, and above all between 1920 and 1930, the expansion continued. Not all of those who had taken refuge in the Paris region from the north returned home. Paris also attracted the wounded or bereaved, since they were given favourable treatment in obtaining posts in the administration, as well as numerous foreigners who either sought refuge from the disturbances of their own countries (Russians, Poles, Armenians, East-European Jews) or who were attracted through the opportunities created by the ever-increasing demands of the Parisian market (such as Italians in hairdressing salons). Many Parisians moved out to the suburbs, believing that to possess one's own house with a small garden was a social advance, and profiting from improving rail facilities. A law of 1919 which restricted work to 8 hours a day gave workers the option of spending more time travelling to work. The métro was extended to many of the bordering communities (a project that was completed by 1937), and the development of a subsidized weekly travelling ticket was a great assistance. The result was that in the department of Seine-et-Oise alone, between 1921 and 1931, the population grew by 50 percent, an increase of 444,000.

Not surprisingly there was much in this experience that was unfortunate. Such rapid growth resulted in the building of large numbers of houses which were ugly and small, in areas which were insalubrious and gloomy, and which were defective in services. Workers found themselves bicycling to suburban railway stations before they began their journey to work, so that between 2 to 3 hours a day were spent in travelling. Many would-be house owners had joined housing-associations, but they were disappointed in the homes that were provided for them. Within Paris itself there was a long-standing housing problem which only became more intense as time went by. The density of the population and the insanitary condition of many of the buildings meant that infant mortality or death from tuberculosis was much higher in the poor arrondissements of the city than in the more well-to-do areas.

Successive governments did little to improve these conditions. Many laws were passed attempting to regulate the relations between landlord and tenant, but within the complexity which they created the only result was to keep the rents low. There were measures to encourage individual construction in the suburbs, but the financial incentives were inadequate and the organization almost non-existent. Part of the political difficulty came from the role of the more conservative Senate, which delayed laws that seemed to extend the role of the state into housing matters or into local government, while other difficulties arose from the antiquated administrative structure of Paris and its region, so that no plan of urbanization could readily be established. The results were movements of protestation. The main one was political, coming from the suburbs, which tended to vote for the left, particularly the Communists, so that Paris was said to be surrounded by a red belt. There was architectural and urbanist protestation from those who thought that the only solution to the deterioration of Paris was to destroy much of what existed and to start again, according to rigid theories. Thus, in 1925, Le Corbusier and others wanted to build some 18 giant towers that would dwarf the historic areas of the city, and would have gutted many districts.

This Paris, with its sad and resentful suburbs, and its overcrowded housing, seems far from the Paris which is traditionally depicted as the home of fashion and the centre of artistic and intellectual life. It remains true that the wealthy and the aristocratic settled in Paris, that it was the seat of the head offices of all the large financial and commercial companies, and that it was the greatest attraction in the world for tourism (Le Bourget airport was handling more than 100,000 passengers a year before 1939). Although there were universities in the provinces, the great and dominant university was that of Paris, which created a large student residential complex to its south, the Cité Universitaire, but which had its vital centre in the Latin Quarter, around the Sorbonne and Saint Germain-des-Prés. Although there were famous writers who lived in and wrote about their provinces (such as Jean Giono, in the Basses Alpes), Paris was to such an extent the meeting place for writers and artists from all over the world that it was accused of draining away the intellectual and aesthetic life of the rest of France. In this way, too, it was claimed that there was a contrast between Paris and the French desert.

But there were other contrasts within Paris, and none more striking than in the co-existence artistically of the traditional and the experimental. There were theatres which specialized in the classics, and the official theatre, the Comédie-Française, was proud of its loyalty to a set presentation of the classical repertoire; there was the theatre of the boulevards which was devoted to light, after-dinner comedies; and there was a group of directors who were producing new plays, bringing on young actors and experimenting with methods of production. The same could be said of novelists and poets, who were divided into those who carried on a traditional type of literature and those who cultivated a sense of revolt or who sought to comment upon contemporary society. There were artists who broke away from the accepted norms and patterns of expression, and who sought to shock and startle the public, philosophers and scientists who rejected rationalist infallibility, architects who used new materials and who created innovations in the exploration of space. They were all accompanied by contemporaries who were more concerned with renewing creation by means of a repetition of what had gone before. The confrontation between the revolutionary and the conservative in culture made Paris a stimulating place, as similar confrontations in politics made it a place of tension.

Paris was also a place of pleasure. One recalls Talleyrand's saying that no one who had not known France before 1789 could know 'la douceur de vivre', and a whole generation claimed that those who had not known Paris before 1914 could not know it at its best. Yet Paris of the 1920s and 1930s has been described as a magnificent and well-equipped fairground. A curious and mysterious writer, Maurice Sachs, who left many recollections of Paris in these years, has stressed the multiplicity and variety of the activities and distractions of the capital.

'The Paris of those days had its Parisians, its painters, poets, philosophers, bars, couturiers, ballets, meetings, politics, religions, actors, musicians, dwellings, photographers, businessmen, select festivities and street fêtes, keen enthusiasms and a young generation that was burning to learn.'

The Parisians, one could say, were in love with Paris, to an excessive, even pathetic, degree. Its charms were too precious to risk their being damaged by the war. In 1940 the French government decided that Paris should be declared an open city and should not be defended against the German invaders. Perhaps in a moment of supreme national crisis the towns and villages of provincial France could be called upon to sacrifice themselves, but Paris was the spoiled child of French civilization. There was also an unhealthy sentimentalism about a Paris which put up statues of Joan of Arc (who was canonized in 1920) and organized parades before them, which loved to decorate the streets with national flags and cockades and to applaud as the walking wounded of the war still marched to the 'fanfares' and drums of countless military bands. Official Paris was something of a dated showplace.

There was also something frivolous and shallow about the achievements of these inter-war years. The representative personages were Coco Chanel, the couturier; several theatrical producers, whose accomplishments were bound to be ephemeral; Cocteau, Louis Moysès (the founder of the nightclub Le Boeuf-sur-le-toit) and Sacha Guitry, most of whose talent was dispensed in the art and ostentation of witty conversation; Picasso and the Surrealists, who sought too desperately to be original and provocative. It could be argued that the greater and weightier figures of the epoch, such as Gide, Proust, Einstein, Freud, Stravinsky, were those whose work dated from before 1914, or who were not, in most cases, specifically the product of Paris.

But Coco Chanel was not merely a couturier; she is important in the history of feminism. The great theatrical producers have created a lasting influence as well as a legend. The varied artistic achievements of Cocteau, as well as his personality, remain exhilarating, and whatever the success today of Sacha Guitry's plays, no one can doubt the importance of his work for the cinema. As for Surrealism, now that it has become a museum piece, one can see how its principles have been constantly reinterpreted and how its long-term effects can still be seen in various contemporary art-scenes, notably in that of the USA. It also represents, by its combination of painting, theatre, literature and photography, the most impressive characteristic of Paris between the wars, which is the totality of its creative commitment.

This Paris of enjoyment started to disappear around 1932. The world economic crisis, which began in October 1929 with the collapse of Wall Street, did not appear to affect France as rapidly as it did other European countries. French industry and agriculture were under-capitalized, based upon small enterprises and small exploitations, and it seemed that they were not so sensitive to international economic movements. In 1930 and 1931 French governments, guided by a conservative with an eye for modernization, André Tardieu, were confident on economic matters and were prepared to introduce forms of social security, including family allowances. But by the end of 1930 French exports and imports were falling and the number of unemployed rising. By the end of the following year it was clear for all to see that the economic crisis had seized France. Industrial production was down, agricultural prices were falling, investments were slumping. Workers suffered from unemployment, the peasantry from a drop in income, investors from a decline in revenue and the government from a decrease in the yield of taxation (as well as from the ending of German reparations).

This economic situation posed a problem which different governments were reluctant to face up to: the value of the franc. As different world currencies were devalued, it became apparent that the franc was over-valued and that this was having a crippling effect on French trade. But there was hostility to any devaluation both on the right and on the left, since it was claimed that the franc was France. Only one statesman, somewhat isolated in political party terms and associated with the centre right, was a clear advocate of the economic arguments in favour of devaluation, and that was Paul Reynaud. The Socialists preferred to think in terms of stimulating demand and of sharing out the work among the labour force, while being reticent about devaluation.

Behind these different appreciations of the economic crisis lay different appreciations of society. The Socialists, for example, attached most importance to unemployment. Their predecessors in government hoped to protect the lower middle class (many Parisian shopkeepers were doing quite well during these years) and the stability of capital. Thus with the electoral success of the Popular Front a wide confrontation of ideals and interest was inevitable.

Even before Blum had formed his government, the month of May 1936 saw the beginning of the greatest wave of strikes that France had ever known. It appeared to be largely spontaneous, often independent of the trade unions (which were always weak in France) and the Communist Party. It used new methods, such as sit-ins, so that hundreds of thousands of workers were occupying factories, department stores and other centres of labour. It was a social explosion which took place in an atmosphere of enthusiasm, even at times of gaiety. This movement expressed the workers' conviction that everything was about to change, that everything was possible (and this was the slogan of one of the left-wing Socialists). Blum profited from the disarray that this caused to employers and to union leaders alike to push through a series of agreements with the employers in June 1936. There were pay rises across the board of up to 15 percent. Trade union rights were recognized and the principle of compulsory collective bargaining established. Most important of all, the 40-hour week and paid holidays were to be enforced by law. It is by this last that the Popular Front has always been remembered: for the first time there were children who were able to visit their grandparents and many French people saw the sea for the first time in their lives.

Other reforms followed. The school leaving age was raised to 14; the organization of the Bank of France was made more democratic; the Leagues were abolished. Eventually, in September 1936, the franc was devalued. But all this was an anti-climax to the heady days of May and June. The economic crisis worsened, the cost of living rose, employers flouted their obligations with impunity, productivity declined. There were many bitter and sometimes violent strikes against the government, which, in an atmosphere of disillusionment, drifted towards its downfall in June 1937. After the customary period of confusion, in April 1938 Edouard Daladier became Premier. His government, like the Radical Party, shifted decisively to the right.

Behind these developments, and dominating them, lay the sinister evolution of the international scene. In 1936 Hitler's troops had re-entered the Rhineland in spite of treaty obligations not to do so. In the same year, although Blum had wished to give military aid to his colleagues in the Popular Front government of Spain, divisions within his government prevented him from doing so and France watched powerlessly while German and Italian intervention ensured a Fascist victory. In September 1938, in order to avoid war, Daladier signed the Munich agreements which obliged France's ally Czechoslovakia to make concessions to Hitler. In September 1939 war came all the same.

The divisions which already existed in French society were not healed by the advent of war. Since the occasion for the international conflict was the German invasion of Poland, there were Frenchmen who wondered whether they should be asked to die for Warsaw; there were those who believed that the solution to Franco-German relations was by agreement rather than by war; some believed that the real enemies of France were the Communists; many Communists believed that the war was being fought for imperialist reasons at the behest of England. Everyone hoped that the war would take place somewhere else than in France and that the horrors of 1914 to 1918 would not be repeated. But on 10 May 1940 the Germans launched their offensive. Many units of the French army fought bravely, but mistakes were made, leaders were pessimistic, the civilian population became panic-stricken. After some four weeks the government abandoned Paris and joined the millions who were on the roads fleeing towards the south. On 14 June the Germans entered Paris.

There were still French people who had illusions, since some believed that it would be possible to live honourably with their German conquerors. But the great period of illusion, which had formed the interlude of the years 1918 to 1940, was over.

The disasters of 1940 were followed by the humiliations of occupation, the calculations of collaboration, the agonies of resistance and the adventures of a Gaullism which was based outside France, in London or in Algiers. These episodes have left an indelible mark on the French people and more than forty years after the Liberation they are still surrounded by controversy and bitterness and they remain a major preoccupation of film-makers, dramatists, novelists and historians who seek through art or through research to assess that which appears impossible to judge. Since all contemporaries seem to have agreed that it was necessary to create a new France, and one which would be totally different from the France that had existed prior to 1939, the inter-war years have become the rejected years. Of course, history is always modifying such condemnations. As French political life has pursued its complexities in the Fourth and Fifth Republics, it becomes impossible to dismiss the politicians of the Third. As creative artists and intellectuals search for that which is fresh and new, and find themselves subjected to the uncertainties of modes and fashions, it is easier to try to appreciate the dazzling abundance of their predecessors of the 1920s and 1930s.

It was always an illusion to think that the whole of western civilization was to be found in the twenty arrondissements of Paris, that artists could escape from reality by being individualistic, that politicians could avoid the unpleasant by being pliant or utopian. But all such illusions persist.

Verdun, 1916. Drawing by Fernand Léger, commemorating France's most devastating battle.

The battle of Verdun is an indelible symbol of the First World War in France. It was not fought for any important strategical reason. The German command deliberately sought a battle of attrition with the hope that it would lower French morale. The Germans believed that the French would feel obliged to fight for the region of Verdun and that they would be bled white. Their losses would be such as to persuade them that the war should be abandoned. The symbolism of the German attack was made all the more obvious because it was led by the German Crown Prince.

The German calculation was proved only too correct in the sense that Verdun became the slaughterhouse of the French and German armies. The battle lasted from 21 February 1916 until 18 December of the same year. No one can be absolutely certain how many men were killed, maimed or gassed, but at the end of the war some 150,000 corpses were collected, and for the next fifty years or so, remains were still being discovered. It seems likely that French losses were between 400,000 and 500,000, with German losses somewhat less.

In French eyes Verdun was a battle unlike any other. In the words of the French commander at Verdun, General Pétain, the town became 'the moral boulevard' of France. Although the population returned afterwards to the town, the surrounding villages found that their land had been destroyed by the bitter and desperate fighting. Nothing would grow; destruction reigned supreme.

Verdun became the embodiment of all the horrors, futility and glories of the war. The phrases persisted: *On les aura* ('We will get them') appeared in one of Pétain's orders of the day, *Ils ne passeront pas* ('They will not get through') became a catchword which was to be repeated when war broke out again in 1939. Somehow the idea grew that if a country could survive Verdun, it could survive anything. Between the two wars France built a greater fortress than Verdun, the Maginot Line, and believed that it was safe.

Verdun became a place of pilgrimage. On Armistice Day, on 14 July, on Joan of Arc's day, or above all on 21 February, the day when the Germans launched the heaviest artillery bombardment that the world had ever seen, those who had fought, *ceux de Verdun*, came in their thousands to remember. In the surrounding villages, and in many villages throughout France, schoolchildren walked in processions to commemorate the battle where, it was said, a French soldier had died every five minutes. The instinctive idea grew that such a battle could not be fought again.

It has been said that war can create considerable social changes. French women, for example, had become active in many sectors, not only as nurses and as farm workers, but also as factory and munitions workers. In the last category it was women who were often the most militant in union activity since they did not run the risk of being sent to the trenches if they threatened to strike, as did their male colleagues. But if women seemed to resume their somewhat effaced rôle after the war, it was because in a war like that of 1914, unlike a war of liberation, the prevailing hope was that once the war was finished everything would return to normal, to the way it had been before the war had started.

A cynic would say that in certain spheres this return to 'normalcy' was achieved. Politics was dominated by two men who had been dominant before 1914, Poincaré and Briand. Conflictual politics became sharper with the foundation of the Communist Party, the strikes of 1919 and 1920, and the organization by the Catholics in the 1920s of a mass movement of protest against the anti-clerical attitudes of Edouard Herriot's government. The strikes in the railways were particularly important and were marked both by their failure and by vigorous repression by the government, which sacked 22,000 railway workers. The immediate post-war period was also notable for certain significant deaths: in 1918 that of Apollinaire, in 1919 that of Modigliani – two precursors of the poetry and the painting of the future. Nineteen-twenty-two saw the death of Proust. In 1924 Anatole France died, a symbol of French literature of the past, a man who had confessed that he found Proust unreadable.

THE **END** OF **WAR**

The war ended when the Germans requested an armistice, which was signed on 11 November 1918. The breaking of the German army was unexpected, and most of the Allied military commanders had not foreseen victory until 1919.

It was fortunate for France when in March 1918 the Germans started an offensive which, after initial success, ran out of steam and permitted the Allies to launch an attack that gave them eventual victory.

For a time it seemed that France was the greatest military power in Europe. The war was seen as a long triumph for the French Army; as a symbol of this, the commander of all the Allied troops in France, Marshal Foch, insisted that the Frenchman who had commanded the army in 1914 and who had been sacked for his failures, Marshal Joffre, should ride beside him in the victory parade of 14 July 1919. Spectators wondered who the peasant in uniform was who shared the honour with Foch.

But if France was victorious, the butcher's bill was a heavy one. In addition to the dead and missing, three-quarters of a million men had been badly wounded.

Opposite, Clemenceau at the tribune of the National Assembly announcing the signature of the armistice on 11 November 1918.

Above, The victory parade led by Foch, in the Champs-Elysées, 14 July 1919.

Left, Parade of the war-wounded, also in 1919.

21

LA FIN de la GRANDE GUERRE

Above, A French cockerel in full cry surrounded by mementoes of French heroism, past and present. Woodcut by Raoul Dufy.

ROMAIN ROLLAND
AUX PEUPLES
ASSASSINES
LIBRAIRIE OLLENDORFF / PARIS

Above, Foch signs the armistice in his train, at Rethondes. Hitler made the French sign the armistice of 1940 in a replica of this same train.

Above, Crowds in front of Maxim's restaurant welcoming President Woodrow Wilson to Paris, 1919.

Left, Woodcut by F. Masereel, 1918, for the cover of a book by the pacifist writer Romain Rolland.

Below, Parade of the War Wounded, (1919). Painting by Galtier-Boissière.

A **SAD VICTORY**

Although the war had been a world war, some of its most terrible battles had been fought on French soil. Almost every family was in mourning. Almost every family had known, through some relative, the hell of Verdun. France was proud in victory, but France's sacrifices were unforgettable. There was hope for the future which, in the eyes of the public (if not in the opinions of politicians) was associated with the prestigious figure of Woodrow Wilson, the American President. These two aspects of the peace remain: all forms of transport possess seats reserved for those who are *mutilés de guerre;* many of the towns of France still have avenues or streets named after President Wilson.

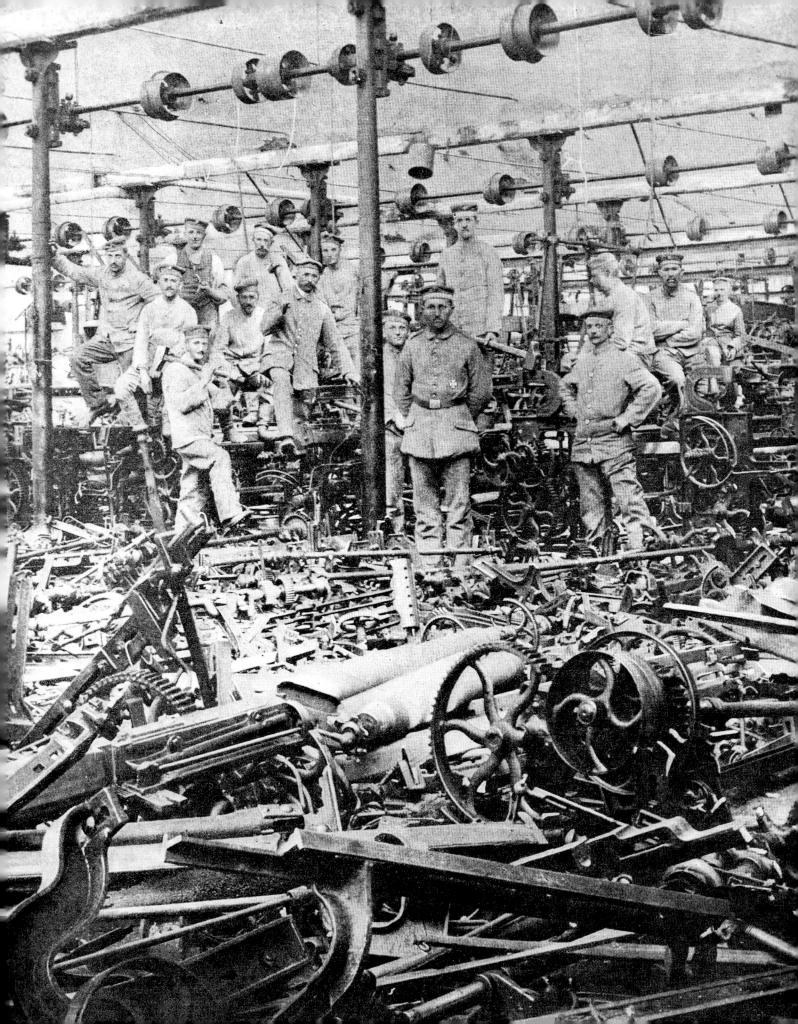

THE **DESTRUCTION** OF **WAR**

France suffered enormously from material destruction. Whole areas had been occupied by the Germans for some four years or had served as a battleground.

Opposite, German soldiers destroying a French textile factory near Cambrai in 1917. This photograph was produced as evidence during the Peace Conference.

Left, The ruins of the town of Verdun.

Below, French cavalry horses grazing in a forest that had been devastated by shell fire.

A GENERATION LOST

As more than 1.3 million French people were killed in the war, the war memorial became part of the scenery of every French town and village. During the years 1919 and 1920, thousands of these monuments were installed and inaugurated. Every 11th of November they formed the centre of commemoration. Sometimes the names of those who had been killed in the 1870-71 Franco-Prussian War were set alongside those of 1914-18 (and some communes have since added to these the names of those who were killed in the Second World War, and in the colonial wars of Indochina and Algeria). But it is always those of the 1914-18 War which predominate. One can stand today in a tiny deserted village and read with astonishment the long list of its inhabitants who lost their lives in those years.

Opposite, The alphabetical lists on many *monuments aux morts* reveal that many families lost more than one member: brothers and cousins, fathers and sons.

Below, The British lost nearly one million men in the war, most of them in France. Thousands were buried in the cemetery at Etaples, near to Boulogne. The famous Blue Train, which carried many British visitors from Paris to the South of France, used to slow down as an act of reverence as it passed the graves.

LIFE IS A DANCING THING

During the war, dancing was frowned on. Governments sought to preserve the image of a patriotic home front, grimly determined in its opposition to the Germans. But the end of the war brought a thirst for enjoyment, and one way in which this showed itself was through dancing. People danced everywhere, in nightclubs, cabarets, restaurants, tea-rooms and cafés – even at home. Clubs sprang up which specialized in the tango (previously considered the most unpatriotic of dances, denounced by the Church, and rumoured to cause psychiatric illness). There were new dances, too: the rumba, the beguine, and the foxtrot vied with the one-step and the shimmy; the Charleston swept Paris with the arrival of the exotic Josephine Baker in 1925. And there were new sounds: American jazz, with mainly black musicians, became a vital part of entertainment.

Above, Jacques-Henri Lartigue photographed his wife, Bibi, dancing the tango with a friend.

Right, Couples dancing to jazz (1920). Illustration by G. Arnoux.

Opposite, Illustration of the famous music-hall, Casino de Paris. Cover design for the magazine *La Joie de Paris* (1930-32).

CASINO DE PARIS

THE BIRTH OF FRENCH COMMUNISM

The Congress at Tours, which began on Christmas Day 1920 as the 18th Congress of the French Socialist Party, turned into the foundation meeting of the French Communist Party when the majority voted to join the Comintern established by Lenin. It has been argued that this split within French Socialism became permanent only because Soviet Russia established close relations with the French Communists, who accepted the Soviet Union as a model. Other factors included the need the Socialists felt for a more forceful role in political and union activities, as well as the Communists' desire that the French should be prepared for the revolutions that were anticipated in several European countries.

Below, Relations between the Communist Party and Soviet Russia had their ups and downs. Two Communist deputies, Marcel Cachin and Vaillant-Couturier, attend a reception at the Soviet Embassy dressed with pointed informality.

Bottom, In 1927 the Communists organized a strike in protest against the death sentence imposed in the United States on Sacco and Vanzetti.

DEUX DÉPUTÉS COMMUNISTES FRANÇAIS ARRIVENT À UNE SOIRÉE DE L'AMBASSADE SOVIÉTIQUE

Voyez, dans ce numéro, le Concours des Monuments, doté de 100,000 francs de prix.

Above, Delegates leaving a meeting at the Congress of Tours on 27 December 1920. The Congress is still that of the Parti Socialiste; the crucial vote was not taken until 29 December.

Left, The future leader of Vietnam, who was to be known as Ho Chi Minh, addressing the Congress and urging that colonial questions be given the importance they deserved.

I.S.R C.G.T.U
Pour sauver SACCO et VANZETTI
TOUS EN GRÈVE DEMAIN

Le Petit Journal

illustré

HEBDOMADAIRE
61, rue Lafayette, Paris

PRIX : 0 fr. 30
28 Janvier 1923

12 Pages

12 Pages

Pour que l'Allemagne paie

L'occupation de la région industrielle de la Ruhr s'est faite sans coup férir. Aux portes de tous les monuments publics et de toutes les usines, les capotes bleues de nos soldats rappellent aux Allemands oublieux les légitimes revendications et la ferme volonté de la France.

GERMANY: ECONOMIC REVENGE IS FOLLOWED BY RECONCILIATION

France believed that Germany would pay for the losses and devastation of the war. In 1920 and 1921 the amount of reparations was fixed, with France awarded the largest share among the Allies, but late in 1922 Germany asked for a suspension of payments. In January 1923 French and Belgian troops moved into the Ruhr to force the Germans to pay. This action achieved some success, but its costs proved ruinous to Premier Poincaré's government. In May 1924 a new government was elected which brought the occupation to an end. Negotiations with Britain and Germany followed, and culminated in the Locarno Pact of 1925 – a mutual guarantee of the French, Belgian and German frontiers.

Above, French troops occupying the Ruhr.

Opposite, The negotiations at Locarno, with Aristide Briand, 'The Pilgrim of Peace' (top), and the German Chancellor Gustav Stresemann (bottom).

Avec ce numéro, LA PETITE ILLUSTRATION contenant
la deuxième et dernière partie du roman : LE SECRET DE LA VILLA DES TROIS CYPRÈS, par M. Albert du Bois.

L'ILLUSTRATION

RENÉ BASCHET, directeur.

SAMEDI 24 OCTOBRE 1925
83ᵉ Année. — Nº 4312.

Gaston SORBETS, rédacteur en chef.

« Les Etats-Unis d'Europe commencent... »
(M. BRIAND, à Locarno, le 16 octobre.)

« Les délégués allemands ont accepté le texte du protocole final non seulement sincèrement, mais joyeusement. »
(M. STRESEMANN, à Locarno, le 16 octobre.)

A LOCARNO, APRÈS LA CONCLUSION DES ACCORDS : LA SATISFACTION DES DÉLÉGUÉS

Photo House. — Voir l'article et les autres gravures, pages 424 à 427.

Jazz, 1925. Detail of a drawing by Raoul Dufy.

France has sometimes been described as 'steadfast and unchanging', and observers have commented on the manner in which its identity is dependent upon the structures which have been established over many years in the past. The new has always existed alongside the old and the traditional. But in the 1920s many people believed that profound and considerable changes were taking place. It did not seem possible that such an event as the Great War could have occurred without such changes following. For philosophers it seemed that civilization itself had been shown to be mortal; for ordinary men it appeared that life could never be the same again.

Foreigners flocked to Paris; opportunities for travel were greatly increased; new fashions in dress became popular; there were different styles in architecture. And if a famous restaurant such as Maxim's remained one of the centres where 'le tout Paris' wished to be seen, it was noticeable that it was no longer the rendezvous of royalty, the aristocracy or the *grandes courtisanes*, but was frequented by the new rich and the more popular figures of the day, such as film stars and sportsmen. Cocktails replaced tea at five o'clock; women took to smoking; and if the Jockey Club continued to flourish, it did so in new premises and in an atmosphere of nostalgia for the past.

Other more obviously important changes took place. A Communist Party was created. A left-wing government (although without the Communists) was formed in 1924. The Locarno Pact seemed to offer prospects for long-standing peace and for an end to Franco-German hostility. The reconstruction of the devastated areas was carried out with great success. The exploitation of petrol, electricity, and chemical products constituted a second industrial revolution, linked to the production of automobiles, the development of the railway system and the growth of banks. The average income rose, between 1913 and 1929, by nearly 40 percent. The supposedly backward entrepreneurs of France found themselves organized into the Confédération Générale de la Production Française.

After military victory, and with artistic dynamism and economic prosperity, was it not possible in the 1920s to suggest that post-war France was progressive as compared with pre-war France? In political terms, however, there was the same instability and ineffectiveness. The left-wing parties fought each other and never achieved their aspirations. The peasants did not participate in the general prosperity and factory workers had to adapt themselves to new methods of production which diminished any meaningful participation by them in the industrial process. Ordinary Frenchmen and women suffered from bad housing and from lack of social insurance. There had been doubts about the solidarity of the franc and when it was rescued by Poincaré many believed that its stability was achieved at the expense of expansion.

Although in the arts the more experimental practitioners were the ones who attracted attention and caused sensation, there were sage literary figures who remained dominant, and whose originality and talent grew from a world of traditional values, such as André Gide, Proust, Paul Valéry and Paul Claudel, while Romain Rolland, Jules Romains and Georges Duhamel set about writing multi-volume novels, *romans fleuves*, which attracted a vast audience.

Perhaps the most revealing episode in this history of change is to be found in the story of *La Garçonne*, a novel published in 1922 by Victor Margueritte. The author, the son of a general and President of the Société des Gens de Lettres as well as a Commandeur de la Légion d'Honneur, had already written several successful and patriotic novels. But *La Garçonne* told the story of a young girl who chose her freedom, breaking away from her fiancé, experimenting with lovers and lesbians, and bearing an illegitimate child. The book was condemned by the Church and banned from bookstalls, and the author was stripped of his Legion of Honour. But in fact, there was no feminist revolution in the years between the wars because what people wanted was a return to the normal pre-war world. Furthermore, after the deaths of so many French men, French women were expected to concentrate on producing children and being good mothers. *La Garçonne* was not in any way typical. Change was both envisaged and experienced, and it was exhilarating, but it was not always profound or lasting.

DADA ANTICS

The war, with its orgy of devastation, inspired forms of literature and art which rejected society's traditional values. One such movement was the short-lived Dadaism. Dadaism had originated in Zurich, where the name Dada (meaning a hobby-horse) had been chosen at random by Tristan Tzara. The Romanian-born Tzara arrived in Paris in January 1920 and was taken up by André Breton, Louis Aragon and Philippe Soupault. The group organized a series of public actions which set out to shock established opinion, both in its view of traditional culture and in its patriotism. Marcel Duchamp, who had returned from America to Paris in 1919, had been attacking traditional art for several years by promoting everyday objects to

the status of art, but though he, like Francis Picabia, was associated with the group and a friend of Tzara's, his involvement was less than whole-hearted. After about eighteen months Breton and his friends realized that Dadaism was essentially negative and broke away to pursue their exploration of the subconscious as a source of creativity, which culminated in 1924 in Breton's first Manifesto of Surrealism.

Opposite
Top left and centre, Cover of the magazine *Le Coeur à barbe* (1922), and a programme for the Soirée du Coeur à Barbe organized by the Dadaists in 1923.

Cover of *Dadaphone* (1920) by Picabia.

Picabia, photographed on the Dada hobby-horse.

Tristan Tzara. Drawing by Picabia.

Opposite
Top right, The revue 391, with a cover by Picabia, celebrating Dadaism and 'instantanéisme'.

Centre, Tzara's play *Le Coeur à gaz,* performed at the Théâtre Michel in 1923, was violently broken up by Breton and his friends. The costumes were designed by Sonia Delaunay.

Bottom left, Disc which creates optical illusions when revolved, designed by Duchamp for his film *Anémic-Cinéma,* 1926.

Bottom right, Headed letter from *Littérature,* founded by Breton and Soupault, which published Tzara's Dadaist manifesto in 1920.

THE MACHINE IN ART

The age of the machine grew out of the war experience. Life became dominated by machinery. Machines and factories created a new landscape, redolent of power, symbolic of the enslavement they could bring to man. Artists discovered the machine as a subject for their art or even as a work of art in its own right. As early as 1915, Marcel Duchamp had signed an iron bottle rack and presented it as 'ready-made' sculpture. Fernand Léger, who had served during the war in an engineering unit, began to use the image of the machine to express modern experience. His precisely executed, mechanical figures stand in machine-like settings. Francis Picabia was among the first to create erotic machine art, which analyzed with wry precision man's more passionate emotions.

Top, Fernand Léger's illustration for *J'ai tué* (1918), an account of the war by Blaise Cendrars. Cendrars, a Swiss by birth who lost an arm fighting in the Foreign Legion, moved in avant-garde literary circles in Paris. Léger here evokes the war machine by his precise delineation of some of war's component parts: helmets, a rifle, signposts.

Right, Max Ernst, *The Roaring of the Ferocious Soldiers* (1919). Ernst lived in Cologne, but was invited to join the Dadaists in Paris after the war and exhibited with them in 1921. Here he takes a playful look at the workings of machinery.

Opposite, Boutet de Monvel's oil painting, *Factory* (1928), captures the massive solidity and dignity of machinery – a more solemn and respectful vision than that of Ernst or Picabia.

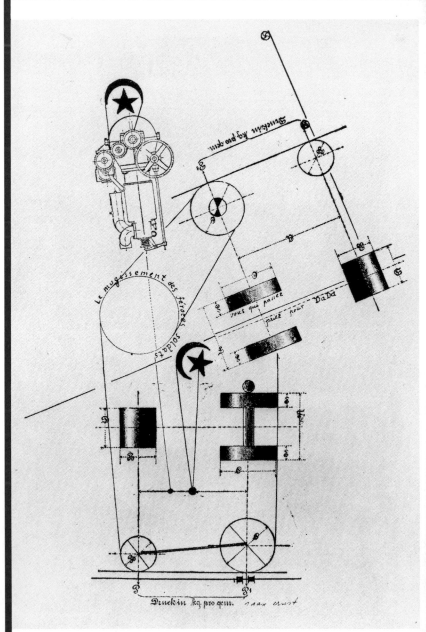

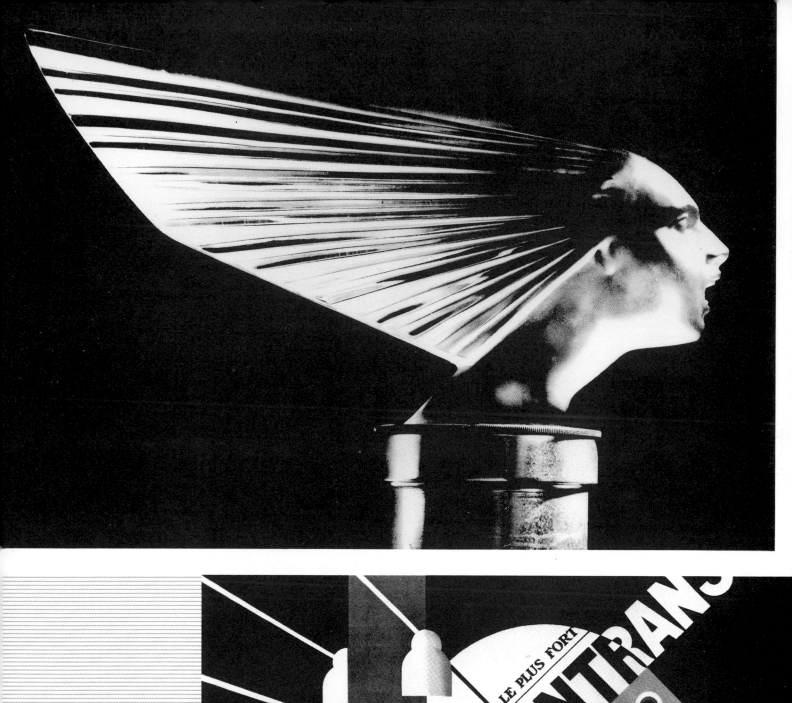

THE NEW CULT IS SPEED

In an age of experiment, one experiment was with speed. It was a period of restlessness: everything and everyone was on the move, a state best symbolized by the motor car. Prior to 1914 the French motor industry had been highly successful and by the end of the 1920s some 250,000 cars were being made in France. Most of these were products of the three leading manufacturers, Renault, Peugeot and Citroën, but speed-lovers preferred American cars, which had a special snob value. A car was seen as an object of beauty, an assertion of luxury. The artist Picabia owned a whole fleet of sports cars. Gertrude Stein had a Ford called Godiva in which she drove the short distance from her home in the rue de Fleurus to Sylvia Beach's bookshop and lending library in the rue de l'Odéon. It became chic to be a man in a hurry, *l'homme pressé.*

Opposite, above, Radiator mascot in glass, by Lalique, 1925.

Opposite, below, Even an advertisement for a small-circulation Paris evening paper, *L'Intransigeant,* had to conjure up an image of speed; poster by Cassandre.

Above, The pleasure of overtaking, design by Guy Sabran.

Left, Advertisement for the American car De Soto, 1925.

Below, In 1926, *L'Intransigeant* again emphasizes its claim for speedy delivery, helped by Cassandre's poster.

NOW THERE IS TIME FOR SPORT

In the early postwar years sport became organized and national. People had more free time (the 8-hour day became law in 1919, the 40-hour week in 1936) and sport became by far the most popular leisure activity for both participants and spectators. The traditional recreations of artisanal culture gave way to commercialized sport (greatly encouraged by the newspapers and the radio). Tennis, athletics, rugby, cycling and other activities seemed to be a liberation from the discipline of the lycée or the constraints of class society. Tennis was particularly important because, as

Simone de Beauvoir recalled, it was the only form of exercise permissible for well-bred young women, and the only sport in which the sexes could meet easily. Paris was the centre of many exclusive tennis clubs. The working class favoured athletics, which did not require expensive equipment or organization. Runs were arranged on summer evenings in the working-class suburbs of Paris and the performance of French runners in the Olympic Games became a matter of national interest.

Far left, Tennis, an undated drawing by Jean Cocteau.

Left, Suzanne Lenglen was only fifteen when she won the French championships in 1914. She won Wimbledon every year from 1919 until 1925, when she turned professional.

Below, left, The Runners, painting by Robert Delaunay, 1926.

Below, Rugby match between France and Ireland, 1927. Rugby was particularly popular in the south of France.

THE FLOWERING OF MONTPARNASSE

Even before the First World War, Montparnasse had been a haven for foreign artists, but it was during the 1920s that it became most famous as a meeting-place for painters, sculptors, writers and musicians. There was hardly a street round Vavin that did not have hotels or studios where artists lived in Bohemian style. Several painters, including Picasso, Chagall, Léger and Soutine, as well as the writer Cendrars, inhabited a quaint circular building called La Ruche, which had been left over from the Universal Exhibition of 1900 and transplanted to the rue Danzig.

The great meeting-places were the three cafés clustered around the Vavin crossroads: La Rotonde, Le Dôme and La Coupole. Cheap meals could be had at Chez Rosalie, in the rue Campagne-Première, where penniless artists sometimes paid with their paintings. Montparnasse meant freedom and congeniality, but the artists sometimes encountered the hostility of xenophobic French people, and relations with the police were not always good. The Surrealists André Breton and Philippe Soupault occasionally met at La Coupole or the nearby Closerie des Lilas (it was there that Modigliani told Breton of his admiration for the poems of Isidore Ducasse which Breton had published in *Littérature*). But Breton disliked the slovenly appearance of the 'Montparnos'.

In the neighbouring rue Huyghens, a society called Lyre et Palette organized exhibitions and concerts. Cocteau and Cendrars read their poems there and Erik Satie and Les Six played their music. Among the many nightclubs was the famous Jockey, where Kiki, with her daring songs and belly dances, became the star.

Above, 'The Montparnos', by Sem, include Kiki smoking a cigarette and Foujita (wearing spectacles) at the table. Foujita was a Japanese artist who drew more often than he painted because he could not afford to buy paints.

Right, Foujita, photographed with two friends in the early 1920s, when he was a symbol of 'les années folles'.

Right, below, Advertisements from *Montparnasse*, 1929.

Opposite, La Coupole with its 'Bar Américain', and the Dôme, both on the boulevard du Montparnasse.

Les „Montparnos"

THE **MONTPARNASSE PAINTERS**

The artists who formed the Montparnasse circle were extremely active in
the years just before and right after
the war. They left an important herit-
age of contemporary portraits.

Opposite
Above left, Moïse Kisling by Chaim
Soutine, *c.* 1925. Kisling was a painter
who had fought during the war in the
Foreign Legion, where he made
friends with Blaise Cendrars. He was
relatively well-off, whereas Soutine
had led a miserable existence, often
giving way to despair and destroying
his pictures.

Above right, Chagall, 1924, a self-
portrait with his wife Bella.

Below left, Leopold Zborowski by
André Derain, 1922. Zborowski was an
art dealer who gave a regular allow-
ance to Modigliani and Soutine.

Below right, Kiki de Montparnasse by
Kisling, 1925. Kiki came from Burgun-
dy and became the queen of the Montparnasse circle. She was Kisling's
favourite model, and he usually represented her with an air of sadness in
spite of her well-known zest for life.
She was also a favourite of Man Ray,
with whom she lived.

On this page
Right, Modigliani, self-portrait, 1919.
Modigliani worked mainly in Paris,
apart from a few months spent in the
south of France after a disastrous exhibition in 1917. The exhibition was
closed by the police because it was
said that his nudes caused offence to
the public, and not a single painting
was sold. But when he died in 1920 (at
the age of 36) there was an immediate
rush for his work.

THE **LOW LIFE**

There were 'houses of pleasure' in every quarter of Paris, supervised by the City Hall and the municipal government. Some were modest; others, mostly located in the city centre, were renowned for their sumptuous decor and were patronized by heads of state and politicians. The brothel Suzy, famous for its discretion, guaranteed its guests total anonymity. The photo-grapher Brassai took these pictures during the 1930s.

Above, Suzy, Rue Grégoire-de-Tours, in the Saint-Germain quarter. Photo-graphed by Brassai, *c.*1932.

Opposite, Hôtels de passe in the Rue Quincampoix. Photographed by Bras-sai, *c.*1932.

SURREALISTS

The origins of Surrealism can be traced back to the 19th-century Symbolists, like Baudelaire, who had rejected constricting rules in order to investigate new areas of experience. The poet André Breton was the movement's theoretician. Having become acquainted with Freudian techniques during his work in a mental hospital at the end of the war, he came to believe that free association of words was more authentic than logical thought. He produced 'Les Champs magnétiques', the first Surrealist text, with Philippe Soupault in 1919, when they practised automatic writing in a state of semi-trance. The artist André Masson applied a similar instantaneous method to his automatic drawings.

Breton issued his Manifesto of Surrealism in 1924. Strongly influenced by the 19th-century poet Lautréamont (Isidore Ducasse), for whom the notion of beauty was the chance meeting on a dissecting table of a sewing-machine and an umbrella, he aimed at discovering a total vision of man by rejecting the limitations of logic. The exploration of the subconscious was all-important, hence the preoccupation with dreams, with chance, with immediacy, *instantanéisme*.

An exhibition of Surrealist work, with paintings by Ernst, Miró, Arp, de Chirico, Picasso, Klee and Masson, and photographs by Man Ray, was held at the Galerie Pierre in 1925.

The cinema appealed particularly to the Surrealists because they saw in the fusion of arts a means of attaining greater authenticity. The Surrealist group disintegrated largely because of political involvements, but their vision continues to affect art and our view of everyday life.

Right above, Page from *La Révolution surréaliste,* no. 1, showing the anarchist Germaine Breton surrounded by various Surrealists and their friends.

Right, Surrealist publications. The cover of *Minotaure,* No. 1, 1933, drawn by Picasso. Most of the cover illustrations for *La Révolution surréaliste,* which first appeared in 1924 to replace *Littérature,* were photographs by Man Ray. *Fantômas* was the name of a series of horror books, published monthly from 1911 to 1914, which became popular in the 1920s.

Opposite, Ready-mades, arranged by Marcel Duchamp. The bottle rack (centre left) was selected on the basis of pure visual indifference.

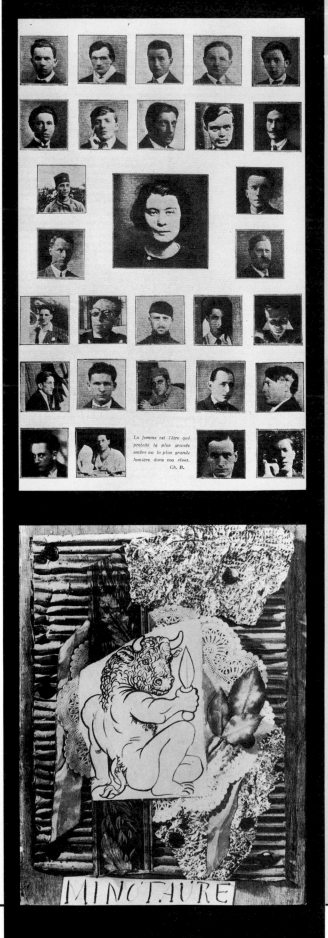

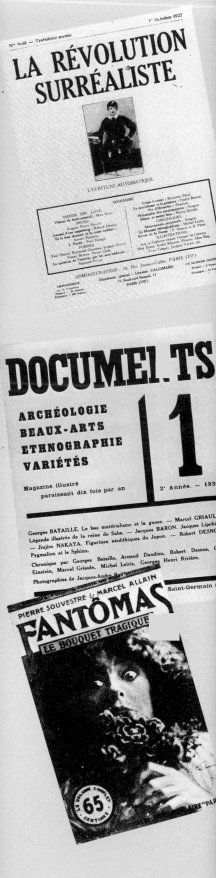

THE SURREALISTS AT WORK

Right above, Salvador Dali, photographed with a star-fish on his head, *c.* 1930.

Right centre, André Breton, *c.* 1930. The spiritual leader of Surrealism, Breton was a man of great integrity who objected to the commercialization of art and literature. He was famous for his three manifestos of Surrealism (published in 1924, 1930 and 1942) and for his novel *Nadja* (1928) – a journal describing his encounters with a mysterious woman in Paris.

Right below, Photomontage of Paul Eluard. From 1919, Eluard was a leading proponent of Surrealism, publishing many volumes of Surrealist poetry. In the late 1930s he broke from the Surrealist movement and during the war joined the Communist Party.

Centre, Sculpture by Alberto Giacometti (1933), who collected objects from the flea markets and sought to confer a magical significance on them by grouping them together in an incongruous fashion. He was expelled from the Surrealist group in 1935 when he began to sculpt from models, eventually developing the individual style for which he is best known.

Opposite, above, Jean Cocteau, *Le Sang d'un Poète* (1930). This is a Surrealist film in which a succession of male and female figures evoke the author's themes and obsessions, and in which the poet himself appears, dramatically draped in a red cloak. Many believed, however, that the film's techniques were too calculated for it to be a true example of Surrealism.

Opposite, below, Salvador Dali, *Evocation of the Apparition of Lenin* (1931). This painting eloquently evokes the semi-hallucinatory quality of Surrealist inspiration.

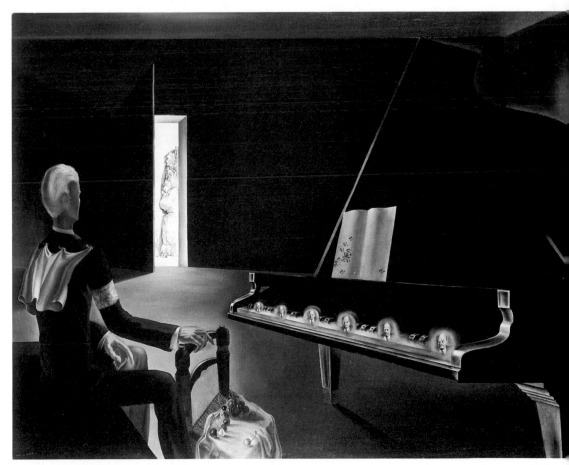

LINDBERGH A RÉUSSI !

L'aviateur a atterri hier soir à 22 h. 25 au Bourget, réalisant

New-York-Paris :

6.000 kilomètres en 33 heures 10 m.

AU BOURGET ET SUR LES BOULEVARDS
LA FOULE ACCLAME
L'INVRAISEMBLABLE EXPLOIT SPORTIF

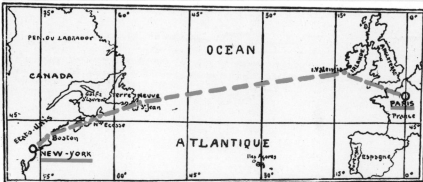

FROM **AMERICA** TO **PARIS**

Everyone knows that when good Americans die they go to Paris. After the war the French capital was a magnet which attracted many nationalities, but most particularly Americans. French people knew America through the cinema – in 1919 there were four times as many American as French films shown in Paris, and with the advent of talkies (films could be dubbed in French from 1930), American cinema became dominant.

Perhaps the two strongest impacts of America on Paris were the heavyweight title fight between Georges Carpentier and Jack Dempsey in July 1921 and the arrival at Le Bourget airport in May 1927 of the 25-year-old Charles Lindbergh at the end of his solo flight across the Atlantic.

Less publicized at the time, but perhaps with a more lasting impact, was the influx of American writers, including Hemingway, Pound, Henry Miller and Gertrude Stein.

Above, Lindbergh and the chart of his flight from New York to Paris.

Right, Scott and Zelda Fitzgerald with their daughter Scottie, in their Paris apartment.

Left, Ernest Hemingway with his compatriot Sylvia Beach, best known for her publication of the Irish writer James Joyce, outside her bookshop Shakespeare and Company. Hemingway's head is bandaged because he had just pulled a skylight down on himself.

Below, Ezra Pound, photographed by Sylvia Beach in her bookshop.

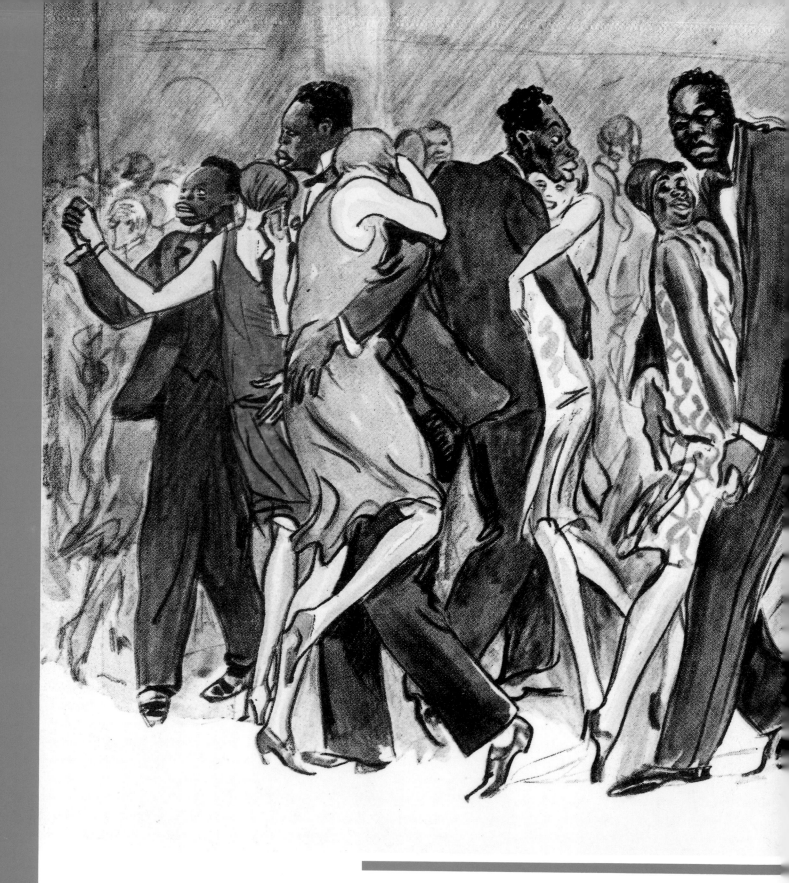

THE **HARLEM** OF **PARIS**

After the war, the Jazz Age came to Paris. The Bal Nègre, the black cabaret in the rue Blomet in the Fifth Arrondissement, was packed night after night. Elegant women would descend from stylish automobiles to dance to syncopated music with handsome young men from the French West Indies or French West Africa. The black vogue was not only a triumph for jazz

Le bal de la rue Blomet.

and the new dance rhythms; it was also a triumph for black culture.

A climax was reached in September 1925 with the arrival in Paris of the American company La Revue Nègre, which played at the Théâtre des Champs-Elysées. The sensational Josephine Baker was the company's star dancer, and Sidney Bechet its leading musician. In the world of Parisian entertainment, nothing would ever be the same again.

Drawing by Sem, 1923.

OPPORTUNITIES FOR TRAVEL

It was sometimes said that the French did not like to travel and preferred to cultivate their gardens. But after the war, great opportunities for travel to distant lands presented themselves. By 1918 the French Air Force had nearly 8,000 aeroplanes, and since their pilots could transfer to commercial companies there were soon some twenty such airlines. The first operated from Paris to London at a cost (in today's money) of around £200 or $300 for a single ticket. The Le Bourget aerodrome was built in the years 1919 to 1924. In 1920 approximately 3,000 passengers travelled by air.

The Ligue Maritime et Coloniale encouraged young people to visit the French colonies and distant countries. Shipping companies were in strong competition with each other.

Right, The Air Express company advertises its Paris to London service, 1920. Soon there were regular air routes: Paris - Strasbourg - Prague - Warsaw, Paris-Brussels-Amsterdam, and Toulouse-Casablanca. It was in 1931 that the pilot Antoine de Saint-Exupéry won the Femina Prize for his novel *Vol de nuit.*

Opposite, Panhard advertises the speed and power of its cars by association with other forms of transport, c. 1930.

FASHIONABLE TRAVEL

It became fashionable to travel to certain places at certain times of the year. In summer the Normandy coast was traditionally the most popular, reached by train in from three to five hours. But the south, too, came into its own (the term Côte d'Azur was in general use from about 1900) and many well-to-do Parisians would set off in December for the casinos and carnivals of the Mediterranean coast. By 1930 places such as Juan-les-Pins, Cannes and Monaco were favoured by those who liked sea-bathing, while the more artistic and intellectual vacationers preferred Vence, Cagnes or Antibes. Biarritz was in a class of its own.

Although winter sports developed slowly in France, by the mid-1920s stylish holidaymakers could be seen from the end of February until mid-March in the mountains of Switzerland (preferably at Saint Moritz) or of France (especially at Chamonix). There they mixed with such personalities as King Albert of Belgium, Queen Ranavalona of Madagascar, and the film star Douglas Fairbanks.

Above, The Deauville seafront, 1926.

Left, Hermès offered fashionable resortwear, as well as a map showing recommended resorts and spas.

Above, Tourists at Lautaret in the French Alps, 1926.

Right, From a contemporary advertisement for the elegant sportsman.

LA VIE SPORTIVE

Women had traditionally been excluded from most French sporting organizations, partly because men tended to use sport as a way of getting out of the house and meeting comfortably together. But there were areas in which women with money and social poise could indulge themselves in sporting activities. Almost a condition of this was that they preserve a particular form of elegance, so that stating their independence went hand in hand with asserting their femininity.

Below, Deauville in 1927. Deauville was famous for horse-racing, polo and bathing. The bathing suit of the woman walking her dog is worn with a net peplos as a promenading costume.

Right, Dressed by Paul Caret, two women stand by their Nieuport aircraft at Le Bourget in 1929.

Below
Left, Golfing costume, 1920. Golf was an upper-class game. France had few golf courses and a woman who played golf in an appropriate costume had made her mark socially.

Centre, Tobogganing fashions.

Right, Ready for take-off in 1922, in a costume by Vionnet, designed for both warmth and elegance.

Just as British and American travellers got used to crossing the Atlantic on famous Cunard Line ships like the *Berengaria* and the *Aquitania*, so the French built massive liners that became equally renowned: the *Ile-de-France*, launched in 1926, the *Paris*, and the *Atlantique*, which accommodated passengers on the South American route starting in 1931.

The outstanding feature of these floating hotels was their luxury. The designers Louis Süe and André Mare, who were best known for their furniture and had founded the Compagnie des Arts Français in 1919, enjoyed their most spectacular success with their *de luxe* cabins and lounges on the *Ile-de-France*.

Far left, above, Cassandre's 1931 poster for the 40,000-ton *Atlantique*.

Far left below, and centre, Artist's rendering of a *de luxe* suite and of the Oval Salon on the *Atlantique*.

Below, Drawing by Georges Barbier, 1928, of typical passengers aboard a French liner.

Right, Normandy beach after 1936.

Below, Leaving for a holiday in 1936, when taking a taxi to the railway station was also a new experience.

VOUS AVEZ PEUR ?—OUI...POUR LE BYRRH!

BYRRH

Above, All means of transport were important for going on holiday. The makers of the aperitif 'Byrrh' cash in on this fact.

Right, Advertisement for a tandem, much used by the working classes on holiday.

Pour faire du tourisme à deux, agréablement sans fatigue, rien ne vaut un TANDEM HIRONDELLE

N° 30C à cadre ouvert

Nº 30C TANDEM HIRONDELLE à 6 vitesses directes		Nº 300C TANDEM HIRONDELLE à 6 vitesses directes
Modèle avec cadre fermé pour le passager arrière		Modèle avec cadre ouvert pour le passager arrière
AU COMPTANT	A CRÉDIT	AU COMPTANT
2000 fr.	280 fr. à la commande et 160 fr. par mois pendant 12 mois	2000 fr.

VACATIONS FOR THE MASSES

France was invaded by the cult of the sun during the 1920s. Until then, it had been the beaches of Normandy and Brittany, mainly Deauville and Dinard, which had been most popular, their casinos and golf courses adding to the attractions of the sea. From 1930 onwards, those who believed that a suntan was healthy as well as chic turned increasingly to Mediterranean resorts.

Because of their proximity to Paris, the beaches of the north and the west were preferred by ordinary working people. When Léon Blum's Popular Front government instituted holidays with pay in 1936, many French families took their first holidays and saw the sea for the first time. The annual holiday became the most important event in the French calendar. Even today, elderly couples relate how, in 1936, they bicycled from Paris to

Brittany and pitched a tent in a deserted field overlooking the sea. When they returned to the same field in 1938 it was so crowded that there was no room for them.

On his return to Paris from captivity after the Second World War, Blum sent a suit to the cleaners. When it came back he found a piece of paper in the top pocket. It read, 'Thanks for holidays with pay.'

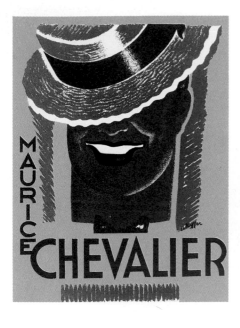

THE MUSIC HALL

In Paris of the 1920s, the music-hall flourished. At the Folies-Bergère Mistinguett reigned supreme. A highly intelligent artist, she embodied the woman from the Paris suburbs, free in speech and manners, but totally devoted to her man, just as Maurice Chevalier, whose career she had launched, represented the debonair Parisian man.

For a few years, the Dolly Sisters enjoyed great success, but Mistinguett's greatest rival was Josephine Baker. Even the Paris intelligentsia flocked to see her. She wore costumes by Poiret, Sonia Delaunay and Schiaparelli, though her most famous attire was a banana skirt.

Opposite, Maurice Chevalier, in boater and bow tie; striking Art Deco poster of Mistinguett at the Casino de Paris; Mistinguett completing one of her famous descents of a grand staircase at the Moulin Rouge, 1927; poster advertising Josephine Baker in the Revue Nègre.

Left, The Dolly Sisters in the 1920s; Josephine Baker in 1929.

Above, Revue des Folies-Bergère, 1926-27, with Josephine Baker (front row, third from left).

THE **EXPERIMENTAL FILM**

At the end of the war French cinema was at a standstill, and the market was flooded by American films. But the period between 1918 and 1929 is important, not because it was a time of many great films, but because a few dedicated cinema enthusiasts succeeded in establishing the value of film as a new art form. One of these was Louis Delluc, who though mainly a theorist of the cinema did produce a handful of films before his early death in 1924. Delluc was the initiator of French impressionism, as opposed to German expressionism, and he was interested in psychology and the manipulation of time. He collaborated with Germaine Dulac, whose Surrealist vision sought to divorce film from other art forms, such as story-telling.

Left, From *Ballet mécanique* (1924) by Fernand Léger, an experimental film exploring rhythm and motion. This strip shows the 'Charlotte' puppet, modelled on Charlie Chaplin, who had achieved cult popularity in France at this time. Léger did several variants on this puppet.

Top, Poster for Chaplin's *The Gold Rush* (1925).

Above, L'Inhumaine. Marcel L'Herbier, one of the period's leading impressionistic directors, made this film in 1923 with Fernand Léger as his set designer.

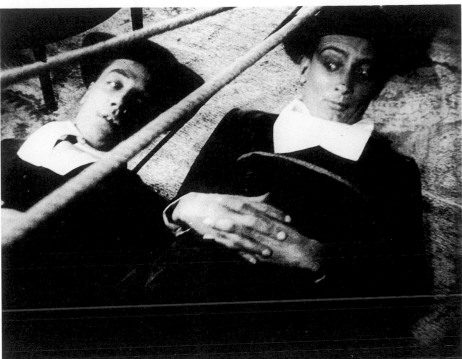

The most considerable innovator was Abel Gance. *La Roue* (1923) achieved powerful effects by its speed and by its contrasting images of landscape, machinery and human faces. In *Napoléon* (1927), the first film ever to be shown at the Paris Opéra, Gance introduced revolutionary techniques, using triple screens and mobile cameras.

The avant-garde movement included Dadaist films such as Man Ray's *Le Retour à la raison*, Fernand Léger's *Ballet mécanique* and René Clair's *Entr'acte*, but the most famous Surrealist film was *Un Chien Andalou* (1928), a series of unrelated, dramatic images put together by Luis Buñuel and Salvador Dali. The most original talent was probably Jean Vigo, who made only three films before his death at the age of 29.

Top left, Albert Dieudonné as Abel Gance's Napoleon.

Top right, Un Chien Andalou (1928) by Buñuel and Dali.

Right, Vigo's satirical documentary, *A Propos de Nice* (1930).

E X P O S I T I O N
INTERNATIONALE
DES ARTS DÉCORATIFS
ET INDUSTRIELS
MODERNES
PARIS, AVRIL-OCTOBRE - 1925

The Exposition Internationale des Arts Décoratifs opened its doors to the public in April 1925. The exhibition had been planned for 1915 but was postponed by the war. Even in the summer of 1925 not everything was ready, and the finishing touches went on long after the official opening. The ten-year delay had the effect of turning what had been meant as a celebration of contemporary style into a retrospective of Art Deco.

Twenty-one countries took part (Germany was not invited and the Bauhaus not represented, though its influence was felt) and everything was on the grandest scale. Fairgrounds, complete with merry-go-rounds, stalls and shooting galleries, contrasted with the elegance of the pavilions of the great Paris department stores which displayed the luxuries of decoration from furniture to fine glass. From afar the Eiffel Tower advertised the name of Citroën in 200,000 dazzling lightbulbs.

Above, Exhibition poster.

Right, A Worth creation being modelled in front of Lalique's illuminated fountains.

Opposite, above, Pavilion of the department store Au Bon Marché.

Opposite, below, Drinks on the terrace overlooking the floodlit exhibition buildings.

Poiret bankrupted himself at this exhibition. His three converted barges, decorated by the Ecole Martine and Raoul Dufy, were lavish showrooms for both his dress designs and interior decorations. However, the public were not interested. Poiret complained that the 'luxury clientèle' had not come, but perhaps he (unlike Lanvin, Chanel and Worth) was displaying a particular elegance whose day was past.

Some pavilions stood out among the mass of Neoclassical buildings because of their modern conception and rich decoration. The master *ébéniste* Jacques-Emile Ruhlmann, who was responsible for the furniture and decorations of the Hôtel d'un Collectionneur, used the most precious, exotic woods, often lacquered, inlaid with ivory, or covered with shagreen. The Pavillon d'un Ambassadeur had a black-and-white lacquered smoking-room designed by Jean Dunand and a study by Pierre Chareau.

Le Corbusier's concrete, steel and glass house for his Pavillon d'un Esprit Nouveau illustrated the ideas he and Ozenfant put forward in their review *L'Esprit nouveau*. It was intended to be reassembled as a dwelling house at the end of the exhibition. Designed as a machine for modern living, the house was the cause of much controversy and spent part of the exhibition surrounded by a fence to render it invisible. 'One thing is sure,' said Le Corbusier, '1925 marks the decisive turning point in the quarrel between the old and the new.'

The transition from élitist to mass production was confirmed by the role of Paris's department stores, many of which offered readymade interiors to the less affluent public.

Top, centre, Place de la Concorde entrance.

Below, Mallet-Stevens's corner of the Pavillon d'un Ambassadeur, with a panel by Robert Delaunay.

Left and far left, Pavillon de L'Esprit Nouveau; interior by Le Corbusier and Ozenfant; detail of exterior by Le Corbusier and Pierre Jeanneret.

FURNITURE

The late 1920s and the 1930s saw an evolution from ornate Art Deco taste to a more functional and modernistic approach. The precious materials favoured by Ruhlmann and Süe et Mare gradually gave way to less expensive woods, metal and glass. Michel Dufet occasionally turned to cheaper materials, believing that 'le meuble de classe' should not remain entirely the privilege of the rich.

Simpler designs evolved. Francis Jourdain proclaimed that one should not buy a chest of drawers in order to furnish a room, but rather for its utility. Le Corbusier was committed to the creation of simple and comfortable designs within the reach of ordinary people. The principle was that an empty room was more elegant than a crowded one.

With the growing use of electricity, much attention was paid to lighting. The review *Luminaire* was exclusively devoted to lamps and chandeliers made of glass, alabaster and metal.

LUMINAIRES
MODERNES
VERRES
DIFFUSANTS

Nouveaux Magasins d'Exposition
4. Av. Pierre-1er-de-Serbie
PARIS (XVIe)

•

Téléphone : PASSY 61-46

•

USINE A BOULOGNE

DAMON

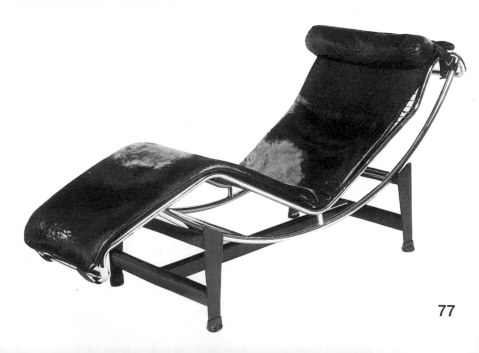

Far left, above, The Grand Salon, exhibited by Süe et Mare at the 1925 Exposition des Arts Décoratifs.

Far left, below, Desk and chair in palmwood and python skin upholstery, designed by Dufet (1930).

Left, Ensemble consisting of a table, a floor lamp in metal and alabaster, and a stool, designed by Pierre Chareau for the Pavillon d'un Ambassadeur (1925).

Above, Advertisement for Art Deco lighting marketed by Damon's studio, including a rotatable desk lamp of 1928 made of nickelled metal by Lacroix (centre), and a Saturn table lamp by Gorinthe.

Right, Le Corbusier's chaise-longue of 1928, designed in collaboration with Pierre Jeanneret and Charlotte Perriand; marketed by Thonet.

77

MODERNISM IN DOMESTIC ARCHITECTURE

Relatively few private houses of architectural significance were built in France between the Wars. Mallet-Stevens's masterpiece is the group of houses dating from 1926/1927 in the Paris street in the Seizième which bears his name. Although each house was scrupulously designed for the use of its particular owner, the whole street gives an impression of harmony. Le Corbusier's houses are expressive of elegant comfort. The Villa Savoye, built in 1929 in Poissy, is a perfect example of his conception of a modern dwelling, with its pillars, wide windows, roof garden and open plan. André Lurçat was an imaginative architect who strove to create an impression of space even when he had to work on very small plots. Such was the case of the Villa Seurat, in the 14th Arrondissement, where he succeeded in building seven houses for his artist friends. Pierre Chareau's Glass House, in the rue St Guillaume, replaced a 17th-century house with a totally new design while leaving a stubborn tenant in her top-floor flat.

Above, The rue Mallet-Stevens, seen from two different angles, 1926-27.

Right, Jean Lurçat's house in the Villa Seurat, designed by his brother André, 1924-25.

Opposite, La Maison de Verre by Pierre Chareau, 1928-31.

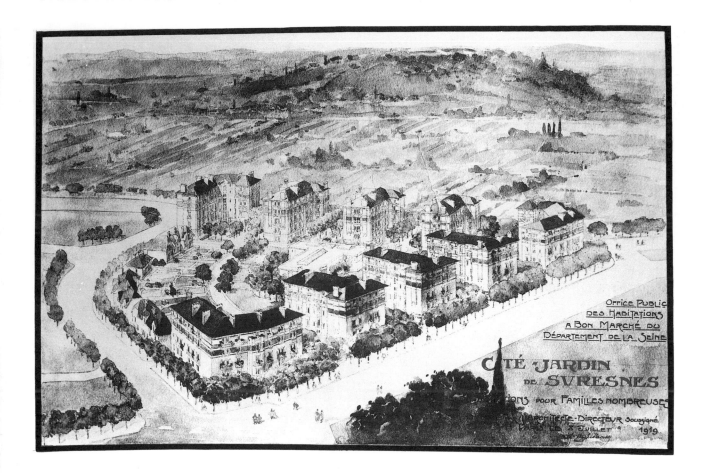

PLANNING FOR THE WORKERS

It is to the Paris region, and to certain provincial cities such as Lyons and Grenoble, that one must look for modern ideas on how to house the ever-increasing French working-class population.

In Paris itself the experience was not entirely successful. Considerable areas of land became available when the old fortifications were destroyed, but these were sold to developers who built high-rise blocks of flats of mediocre quality. In the expanding suburbs, too, many municipalities allowed housing to spread incoherently wherever profits were to be made. But others, usually left-wing in politics, attempted to organize architects and engineers on socialist lines. Boulogne-Billancourt enlisted Le Corbusier, and the Cité de la Muette in Drancy, Lods and Beaudoin.

The greatest innovation, however, was the introduction of the garden city beginning in the 1920s. The most interesting, because of the originality of its plans and its subtle mixture of working-class and middle-class dwellings, is that of Suresnes, which was built under the supervision of Maistrasse and Quoniam.

There were remarkable architectural achievements in Lyons, where the district des Etats Unis was created. In the Lyons suburb of Villeurbanne a district of skyscrapers was developed by Giroud and Leroux in 1935. Its belfryed town hall and 18-storey blocks of flats formed an entire new town.

Opposite
Top, The Cité Jardin of Suresnes, 1919.

Centre, The Cité Jardin of Drancy, 1920.

Left, La Cité Jardin des Lilas after 1920.

On this page
Above, Boulogne-Billancourt.

Right, The Municipal Theatre of Villeurbanne, opposite the Town Hall.

In 1919 a competition was launched for a development in the Paris region. As usual, there was controversy between those who wanted to preserve Paris and those who wished to create a 'rational' and 'functional' redevelopment. Among the latter, Le Corbusier drew up a revolutionary vision, the Plan Voisin. This would have destroyed the centre of Paris and housed its population in 18 identical towers.

The competition for the development of the hill of Chaillot led to designs on almost as monumental a scale: Sauvage's pyramidal blocks, Le Corbusier's towers flanked by lower buildings, and Mallet-Stevens's ingenious combinations of geometrical shapes. Perret's plan envisaged a wide vista of low buildings, accompanied by massive towers.

The more visionary schemes were never carried out, partly because of the financial crisis of the 1930s, and partly because the authorities were reluctant to accept the new 'International Style'. The Cité de la Muette in Drancy was one of the few schemes to be realized.

Left, Perret's design for tower blocks (1928).

Below, Sauvage's plans for the redevelopment of the Porte Maillot (1931).

Opposite, above, Lods and Beaudoin: the Cité de la Muette, Drancy, in eastern Paris (1935; now demolished).

Opposite, below, Le Corbusier's plan for Paris (1925).

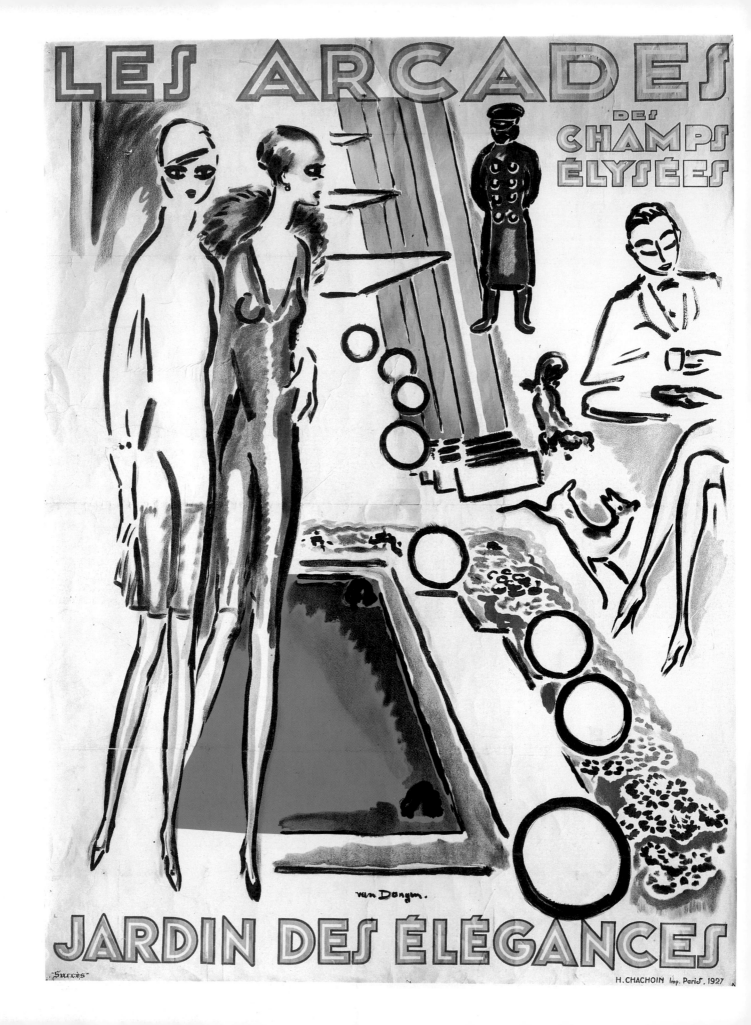

LE **SHOPPING**

Opposite, The elegant arcades of the Champs-Elysées, depicted in Van Dongen's 1922 poster.

Below, Sonia Delaunay did much to revolutionize taste in fashion as well as design. Her boutique, in collaboration with Jacques Heim the couturier, opened in 1925 and closed in 1929, just before the crisis.

Right, Big stores helped bring the new lifestyle to the masses. Anything could be bought at La Samaritaine – from garments to furniture, household goods, and sports equipment. This is one of two buildings added to the store between 1928 and 1930, designed by Francis Jourdain and Henri Sauvage.

Below right, Hairdressing salons proliferated. The new short hairstyles required regular attendance, as did the fashion for wavy hair which made the Eugène perm a woman's best friend. The elaborate Art Deco style of this salon contrasts sharply with the pared-down modernity of Delaunay's boutique.

Théàtre de la Gaîté-Lyrique

× × ×

QUATORZIÈME SAISON RUSSE

× × ×

SOIRÉES DE GALA DE

Ballets Russes

DE SERGE DE DIAGHILEW

× × ×

MAI 1921

Serge Diaghilev's Ballets Russes changed the face of ballet in Paris in 1913 with their first performance of Stravinsky's avant-garde ballet *The Rite of Spring,* choreographed by Nijinsky. Revived in 1920, with choreography by Massine, the ballet's influence was considerable, undermining the romantic tradition and emphasizing colour and exoticism. Stravinsky's *Pulcinella* was performed in the same year and his *Apollon musagète,* a suite of dances in Neoclassical style, in 1928.

Diaghilev drew on the talents not only of his dancers but also of the writers, musicians, painters, and designers of his era. For *Le Train bleu,* for example, Chanel contributed costume designs; Cocteau wrote the scenario; and Darius Milhaud the music.

In the mid-1920s the Ballets Russes declined and the company gave its last performance in Paris in 1929. Later that year Diaghilev died, but his aesthetic impact survived him.

Opposite, Le Train bleu, 1924, with Lydia Sokolova, Anton Dolin, Nijinska and Leon Woizikowsky. Swimming, golf, tennis and acrobatics featured in this sporting ballet set on the Riviera.

Above, Serge Lifar and Alexandra Danilova in Stravinsky's *Apollon musagète.*

Left, Programme for the Ballets Russes, by Picasso.

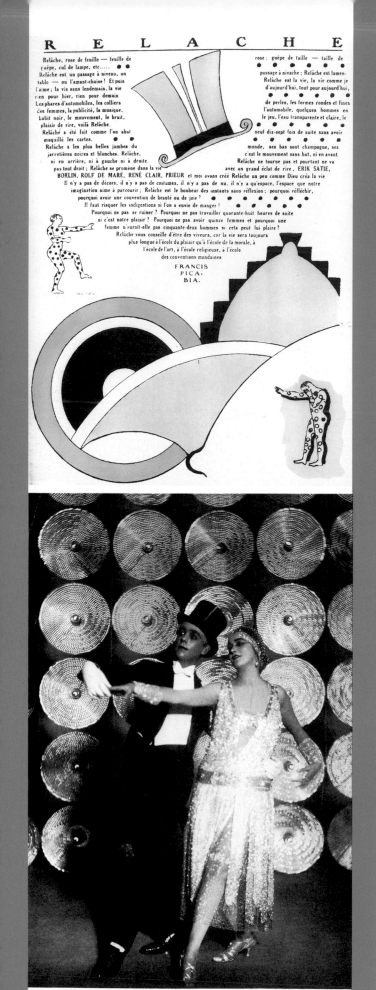

THE
BALLET SUEDOIS

Rolf de Maré, a wealthy Swedish art collector, founded a ballet company after the war in collaboration with Michael Fokine. Like Diaghilev before him, he commissioned great artists – Bonnard, Léger, Picabia and others – to design the décors. In 1921 de Maré produced *Les Mariés de la Tour Eiffel*, a mime play with scenario by Cocteau and music by Les Six. The star was

Jean Börlin, a young Swedish dancer, who enthralled Paris audiences with his grace and athleticism.

Much of de Maré's work was done in collaboration with Darius Milhaud. After *L'homme et son désir*, with a scenario by Claudel, Börlin choreographed *La Création du monde*, a Negro ballet written by Blaise Cendrars, based on African legend.

In 1924 Picabia commissioned de Maré to produce *Relâche*, with music by Satie and an interlude comprising a film by René Clair, *Entr'acte*. The ballet was given a rowdy reception.

Finding no new paths to explore, and unwilling to repeat himself, Rolf de Maré disbanded his company in 1925, but it was he who welcomed the Revue Nègre to Paris in the same year.

Above, **La Création du monde**, 25 October 1923. Music by Milhaud; curtain, costumes and scenery by Léger.

Opposite, above, Programme cover by Picabia for *Relâche*, 1924.

Opposite, below, Jean Börlin and Edith von Bonsdorff in *Relâche*.

CLOWNS

The circus was hugely popular and attracted people from all walks of life. Les Six used to accompany Cocteau to Medrano, to watch Paris's best-loved clowns, the Fratellinis, whose technique was so admired that Jacques Copeau invited them to teach movement at his drama school.

Sacha Guitry had spent his childhood in Saint Petersburg, and was enchanted by Douroff, the clown, mime and illusionist. One of Guitry's earliest and most successful plays was *Debureau*, in which he revealed his admiration for those who express their feelings through their bodies rather than through words. The Prologue to the play represents the circus parade at the Théâtre des Funambules in 1839.

Opposite, above, Yvonne Printemps with her husband Sacha Guitry in *Debureau,* 1918. In the play within the play, Debureau's son offers to replace him when he can no longer act.

Opposite, below, Pierrot and Harlequin, by Picasso, 1920.

Left, Two Pierrots by Juan Gris, 1922.

Below, Grock was an immensely popular clown of Swiss origin, who carried a tiny violin in a huge case. Drawing by Bib.

Since Watteau's *Gilles,* painters have been attracted to the characters from the Commedia dell'Arte. Picasso, who never went to the theatre, visited the circus several nights a week. He and Juan Gris painted a notable collection of melancholy Pierrots, Harlequins and mountebanks.

L'ÉVOCATION FIDÈLE DES MAÎTRES DISPARUS

LES PLUS BRILLANTS ORCHESTRES AUX RÉUNIONS MONDAINES

LE **PHONOSFER 12**

"Radiola"

79, Boulevard Haussmann. Paris

the 'Minuit Chansons' establishments, where a coin in a slot produced a popular song. When nightclubs started to close in the 1930s, people danced at home to the gramophone, and the accessibility of music added to the general gaiety of the sit-ins during the 1936 strikes. The vogue for *surprise parties* spread among adolescents, and the unexpected arrival of a group of friends, equipped with records, would lead to an evening of music and frantic dancing.

The recording of serious music was delayed for technical reasons. But in 1926 Columbia recorded Stravinsky's *L'Oiseau de feu,* despite his quip that 'la musique, c'est fait pour être vu.' The conductor Toscanini, who had for ten years refused to make records because he was not certain of having an uninterrupted session, was recorded for the first time in 1935.

Left, Advertisement for the gramophone (1930).

Below, Advertisement for Pathé records, by Cassandre.

Opposite, right, A family gathering. Photograph, 1925.

Opposite, below, Minuit Chansons, Montmartre, 1931. Painting by Edward Burra.

POPULAR MUSIC

The wireless set and the gramophone provided easy access to music. From 1920 onwards the radio was the centre of the home and housewives escaped the lonely dreariness of chores by listening to Sacha Guitry, Gaby Morlay, Mistinguett, Maurice Chevalier or Lucienne Boyer.

Middle-class women invited each other to tea and listened to the radio together. The famous commentator Marcel Laporte, known as Radiolo, was almost part of the family. His station, Radiola, later became the state-owned Radio Paris, through which the government exercised considerable influence. In 1935 radio advertising was launched – an important event in view of the five million radio sets owned in France by 1938.

The record industry prospered. Families gathered reverently round their loudspeakers, or went out to visit

Pathé

L'ENREGISTREMENT ÉLECTRIQUE LE PLUS PE

M. Marcel Proust est mort

M. Marcel Proust, qui était venu assez tard à la littérature (il n'avait guère écrit avant l'âge de quarante-cinq ans), est mort. C'est peu d'années avant la guerre que son nom franchit le cercle de ses amis quand il publia le premier ouvrage de sa série *A la recherche du temps perdu : Du côté de chez Swan,* lequel fut suivi coup sur coup de *A l'ombre des jeunes filles en fleur, Du côté de Guermantes* (2 volumes) et de *Sodome et Gomorrhe* (2 volumes). Il annonçait, toujours dans la même série, un troisième et un quatrième *Sodome et Gomorrhe,* puis *Le temps retrouvé.*

Paris fait à Anatole France de splendides funérailles

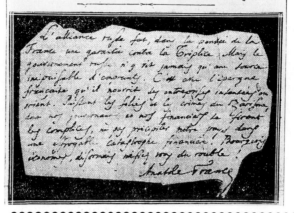

VICTOR MARGUERITTE

La garçonne

ROMAN
II

Collection "L'Amour"
4 fr. 50
FLAMMARION

Collection Alter Ego

M·L.

La Rose de François
poëme inédit par
JEAN COCTEAU

75

Select-Collection

COLETTE

Chéri

ROMAN

E. FLAMMARION, Éditeur, 26, rue Racine.

LITERARY LIONS

French literature has always been noted for its diversity. Tradition, controversy and innovation are all easily joined. Within the tradition of Balzac and Zola fall the novel sequences known as *romans-fleuves*, which depicted the lives of a family and its descendants, and which bore testimony to the fidelity of the reading public.

Opposite
Above left, The Communist newspaper *L'Humanité* announces the death of Marcel Proust in November 1922. While praising his genius and originality, it regrets what it calls his tendency to enter into 'détails parfois inutiles'.

Above right, Extract from a manuscript by Anatole France published by *L'Humanité* on the occasion of France's funeral in 1924.

Below left, Cover of the third edition of Victor Margueritte's *La Garçonne* (first published in 1922), a novel about an emancipated woman which caused a scandal.

Below centre, Marie Laurençin illustrates Cocteau's poetry in 1923.

Right, Cocteau's drawing of his literary discovery Raymond Radiguet, who died in 1923 at the age of 20. Radiguet wrote two masterpieces, *Le Diable au Corps,* a novel about a love affair between an adolescent and the wife of a serving soldier, and the posthumously published *Le Bal du Comte d'Orgel,* an allegory of contemporary society.

Below right, Colette's *Chéri* (1921), the story of an aging *grande courtisane's* love for a feckless but beautiful young man.

On this page
Above, Caricature of Jules Romains, by Czerclkow, 1927. This prolific writer of novels, poems and plays was best known for the 27 volumes which formed his *roman-fleuve, Les Hommes de bonne volonté* (published between 1932 and 1947).

Left, Roger Martin du Gard, whose long novel sequence, *Les Thibault* (1922-40), won him the Nobel Prize in 1937.

Below, Romain Rolland was famous before 1914 for his 10-volume *roman-fleuve, Jean Christophe.* After the war he wrote a 7-volume novel, *L'Ame enchantée,* and many works on pacifism, Communism and Buddhism, as well as sketches of Burgundian peasant life, in *Colas Breugnon* (1919).

Mistinguett sings to striking workers, 1936.

Historians like to divide French history into different periods, and do not agree on what these periods should be. But all recognize that from 1930 onwards there is a time of troubles, and that from 1936 – the coming to power of the Popular Front – there is a wave of divisiveness, bitterness and pessimism that affects all sections of the population.

It is possible to explain this in economic terms. The prosperity of the 1920s, the protected position of a France which had a strong currency and a resilient peasantry, which was famous for luxury goods and preferred above any other by tourists, all faded away as the depression took effect in France. The experience of the Popular Front suggested that Socialist remedies were no more successful than those of more orthodox governments. If France was the last important European country to be affected by the economic crisis, it was also the last to recover from it. The decade of the 1930s has been compared to the defeat of France by the Prussians in 1870. It was France's economic Sedan.

It is also possible to explain the situation in more purely political terms. Briand died in 1932, Poincaré in 1934, and although Herriot remained an important political figure, he never again became Premier after his six-months government of 1932. Therefore France was largely governed by new men, most of whom failed to impose themselves on political opinion, as their predecessors had done. The most distinguished and famous, Léon Blum, had not held any ministerial office until he became Premier in June 1936.

The confused political situation was influenced by what was happening beyond the French frontiers. There were Frenchmen who believed that the answer to France's ills was to follow the example of Fascist Italy or Nazi Germany, while those who favoured the Soviet model were all the more disposed to follow it as a means of protecting themselves from Fascist threats. Hatreds developed: some blamed unpatriotic Communists, international Socialists and Freemasons, foreigners and Jews, for all the misfortunes that befell France; others blamed the small clique of rich families, the privileged who were determined to keep the lower classes in their place and who looked after their own interests rather than those of the nation.

There was a reluctant realization that the destiny of France would not be settled by deciding whether to support Edouard Daladier or Edouard Herriot, 'les deux Edouards' of the Radical Party. When it was pointed out that the French population formed only slightly more than 7 percent of the population of Europe these figures were greeted with indignation, but it was recognized that the future depended upon what was happening in Berlin, Rome and Moscow. And if France was to avoid war, for which her army was preparing but which her army did not want, much would depend too upon what happened in London.

France, reduced to her own economic and diplomatic dimensions, suffered also from a lack of cultural inventiveness. It was in referring to this epoch that someone remarked that for four years Gide had produced no work of any importance and that nobody had noticed. The greatest literary sensation before the war was *Gone with the Wind*, by Margaret Mitchell, which, after much hesitation, the august literary firm Gallimard published. The most gifted writer was Céline, but few critics discerned the talent that lay beneath his violent and obsessive denunciations of Jews, Communists and the French bourgeoisie, even though he was expressing a certain climate of opinion. Writers and critics, like politicians and economists, were ill-at-ease and uncertain. In 1938 Jean-Paul Sartre published his first novel, *La Nausée*. It too denounced the bourgeoisie, but its discussion of existence and reality was complex. This work was expected to win one of the great literary prizes, but instead the prize in question went to a novel that is now totally forgotten, an event which is typical of these years.

J. SENNEP

Unis comme au franc !

THE FRANC IS FRANCE

It has often been said that the French bourgeoisie would rather give its sons in war than give up its gold. The war was financed by expensive loans rather than by taxation, and the same was true of the reconstruction of devastated areas of the country. For a time it was believed that reconstruction would be paid for by the Germans, but this soon proved to be impractical. So French governments allowed inflation to proceed. Prices rose and confidence in the franc fell. The value of the franc on the international money market declined and there was a flight of capital from France, with the result that in the mid-1920s a series of government crises arose out of the crisis of the franc. When Poincaré became Premier in July 1926 he set about revaluing and stabilizing the franc, which then became sacrosanct. To devalue further was considered unpatriotic, and during the world economic crisis of the 1930s this solution was ruled out for France. When Pierre Laval carried out his policy of deflation in 1935, reducing government expenditure to maintain the franc's value, he was accused of prolonging the economic slump.

Opposite, Masereel's view of inflation in a woodcut, 1920.

Above left, Cartoon by Sennep of Poincaré's government in 1929.

Left, Caricature of Laval in self-congratulatory mood in 1935 after saving the franc and thus stifling the criticisms of his opponents Marcel Cachin (Communist) and Léon Blum (Socialist), depicted behind.

Above right, Le Petit Journal for 4 July 1920 compares pre-war and post-war prices of clothing for women and priests.

— Maintenant que tu es hors d'atteinte, ils peuvent bien dire de moi ce qu'ils voudront.

After the 1932 elections the Radical Party held the balance between left and right in the National Assembly. A number of financial scandals occurred in which members of this party were implicated, but it was the 'affaire Stavisky' that caused most reverberations. Towards the end of 1933, Stavisky, a financier of dubious reputation, was found not only to be guilty of fraud, but to have been protected by various politicians, several from the Radical Party. Stavisky went into hiding, and on 8 January 1934 was found dying, supposedly by his own hand. It was widely suspected that he had in fact been murdered, to prevent him from making revelations about his highly placed political friends. The Radical premier resigned and another Radical, Edouard Daladier, replaced him. In order to win Socialist support, Daladier dismissed the Paris Prefect of Police, Chiappe, who was alleged to treat right-wing demonstrators favourably while being hostile to those of the left. The result of the Stavisky scandal and of the Chiappe dismissal was the right-wing demonstration of 6 February 1934, at which the police were forced to fire into the crowd, killing 14 people and wounding more than 200. The next day, despite his parliamentary majority, Daladier resigned through fear of further violence. The left replied with a one-day general strike, supported by both Communists and Socialists. The violence of the right seemed to herald Fascism, the union of the left the Popular Front.

Opposite, above left, 'Parlons Français'. The Republic contemplates the gaming table where 'rien ne va plus', because of the 'affaire Stavisky'. Cartoon by Iribe.

Opposite, above right, The dummy of Stavisky (also known as Monsieur Alexandre) is installed in the Musée Grévin.

Left, The riots of 6 February 1934.

Top, The crowds in the Place de la Bourse learn of the resignation of Daladier on 7 February 1934.

Above, The Socialist newspaper *Le Populaire* celebrates the success of the one-day strike of 12 February 1934, which it hails as a victory over Fascism.

UNEMPLOYMENT AND PROTEST

The Wall Street Crash of 1929 did not immediately affect France. Self-financing firms, small agricultural enterprises, and the stable Poincaré franc suggested that the country was safe. But from 1931, trade declined and a huge overseas deficit developed. Production dropped, share-values fell, bankruptcies became more common, and agricultural incomes declined. Unemployment increased severely, reaching a quarter of a million by 1932. Among the middle classes, even groups like shopkeepers and civil servants, who were protected by the government or who profited from the general fall in prices, felt anxiety about the future. France became a country of apprehension and protest.

Opposite, Outside a labour exchange in 1930, when unemployment first began to rise.

Left, 'Le Calvaire', 1934: France is crucified by the depression. Chanel is said to be the model for this image of France.

Below, A workers' demonstration in 1930, organized by the Confédération Générale du Travail. Placards castigate 'les cumuls' – those who have more than one job.

LE CALVAIRE

THE **POPULAR FRONT**

Following the Fascist threats of February 1934, the Communists and Socialists agreed upon unity of action and were joined within a few months by the Radicals. By 1935, intellectuals, trade unionists and political leaders were using the phrase 'Popular Front' to describe the broadly based left-wing movement which opposed the Fascist leagues and aimed to end the economic crisis and establish greater social justice. Huge rallies and demonstrations were held all over France in preparation for the elections of spring 1936. The result was a victory for the Popular Front coalition (and particularly a notable increase in the number of Communist deputies elected). As leader of the Socialist Party (the largest in the Assembly), Léon Blum became leader of the government. But before he assumed power, France experienced its largest movement of working-class protest. In resolving this crisis, the Popular Front government achieved its most famous reforms: holidays with pay, the 40-hour week, compulsory collective bargaining, and pay rises. The formation and early days of the Popular Front were moments of great enthusiasm and confidence.

Above, Design for a float in 1936, by Marcel Gromaire and Jacques Lipchitz, showing the Popular Front continuing in the tradition of Zola, champion of miners and peasants.

Right, Socialist and Communist leaders in 1936 at the traditional pilgrimage to the spot in the Père-Lachaise cemetery where members of the Paris Commune of 1871 were shot. In the centre is Léon Blum, with the Communist leader Maurice Thorez on his right and Marcel Cachin on his left. On the extreme right, holding his hat, is perhaps the most important of the Communists, Jacques Duclos.

Opposite, One of the early demonstrations in favour of the Popular Front and its opposition to Fascism, held on 14 July 1935.

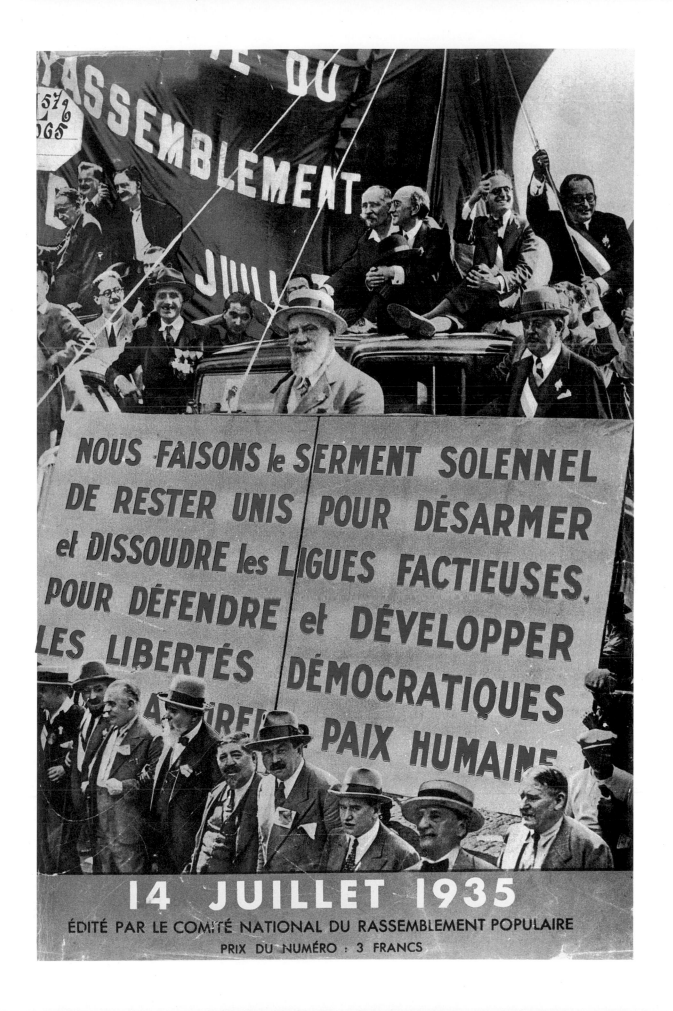

NOUS FAISONS le SERMENT SOLENNEL DE RESTER UNIS POUR DÉSARMER et DISSOUDRE les LIGUES FACTIEUSES, POUR DÉFENDRE LES LIBERTÉS et DÉVELOPPER DÉMOCRATIQUES PAIX HUMAINE

14 JUILLET 1935

ÉDITÉ PAR LE COMITÉ NATIONAL DU RASSEMBLEMENT POPULAIRE

PRIX DU NUMÉRO : 3 FRANCS

THE SPANISH CIVIL WAR

The Popular Front was destined for many disappointments and disillusionments, and was to cause much bitterness. This was inevitable, given its policies and aspirations, and given the expectations that it had engendered. But the impact of the Spanish Civil War could not be foreseen. When, on 20 July 1936, Léon Blum was asked by the Spanish Prime Minister for help in putting down an insurrection which had started two days earlier, it seemed natural that Blum would agree to help another Popular Front government. But his cabinet was divided and many of his own supporters, as well as his ally the British government, advised him to follow a policy of non-intervention. There appeared to be a danger of international war over Spain, and moderate Socialists and Radicals shrank from becoming involved. But the Communists and the left of the Socialist Party complained bitterly that their Spanish comrades were being abandoned to the Fascists. The habit of popular agitation and demonstration that had previously worked in Blum's favour now turned against him.

Above, Poster by Miró, 'Help Spain'. Miró wrote that in the Spanish struggle he saw on the Fascist side the forces of the past, and on the other side the people whose resources would give Spain a move forward that would astonish the world.

Left, Refugees arriving at the Spanish-French frontier.

Opposite, Sketch by Picasso made in 1937, in preparation for his great mural *Guernica,* which commemorated the bombing of the Basque town by the Germans. *Guernica* was exhibited by Picasso at the 1937 International Exhibition and was the most publicized artistic protest against General Franco and his German and Italian allies.

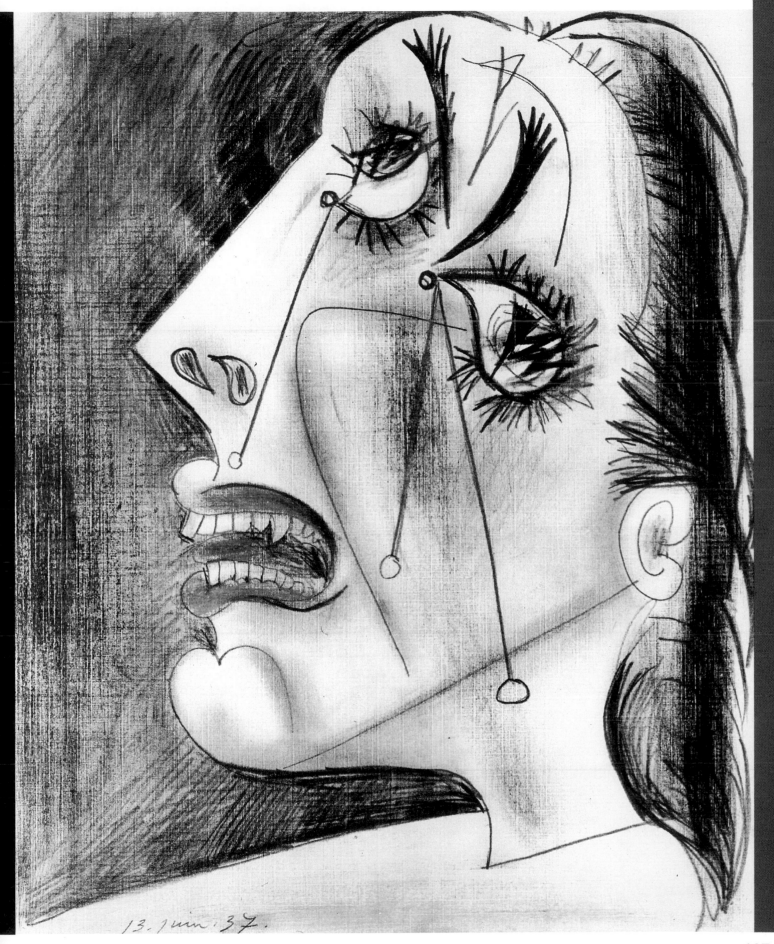

13. juin 37.

MALRAUX AND SPAIN

The novelist André Malraux had been in Spain immediately before the Civil War, and when the war broke out he organized an air squadron of volunteers and mercenaries to help the Republic. For the next few months Malraux shared the passion of Spain, and his subsequent writings and speeches, and eventually his film-making, had an enormous influence on French response to the Civil War. At meetings in France and America, Malraux impressed his audiences both as a personality and as a writer committed to action. His burning idealism, linked to his sense of adventure, made him a unique and charismatic figure. *L'Espoir*, Malraux's novel about the Spanish Civil War, appeared in 1937 (though it did not have Picasso's *Guernica* sketches, as had once been planned). The film of the novel was completed in 1939 but was not shown until 1945.

Below, A scene from the film *L'Espoir,* which Malraux describes as a true episode. A plane from his volunteer squadron had been brought down among mountain villages. The whole local populace followed the stretcher bearers as they brought the wounded airmen down the mountainside. When Malraux raised his eyes, the file of peasants extended from the heights of the mountain to its base. It was, he said, the greatest image of fraternity that he had ever encountered.

Opposite, Malraux in Spain, and a poster for the film *L'Espoir.*

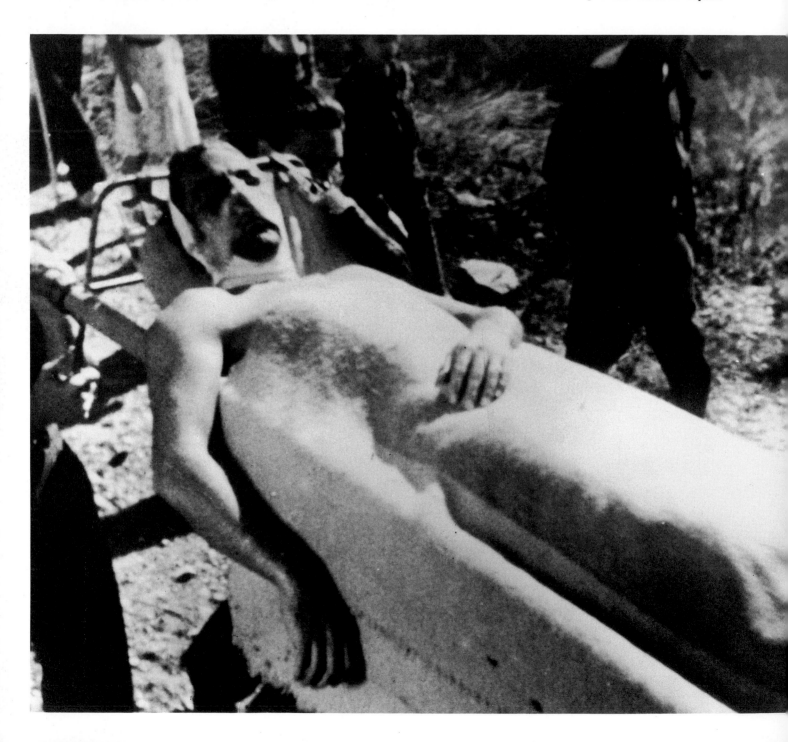

LE
MOUVEMENT DE LIBÉRATION NATIONALE
présente
ESPOIR
SIERRA DE TERUEL
Un film d'ANDRÉ MALRAUX
Musique de DARIUS MILHAUD
Une Production CORNIGLION-MOLINIER
Réalisé en Espagne pendant la guerre civile

For Parisians, the years immediately before the war were marked by several celebrations. The first was the International Exhibition of 1937. This exhibition was supposed to be inaugurated on 1 May as a celebration of modernization, with some fifty different countries displaying their buildings and advertising some of their national achievements. But the gigantic site, opposite the Eiffel Tower, which would have as permanent buildings the Palais de Trocadéro and the Musée de l'Art Moderne, was the scene of bitter labour disputes. In spite of the appeals of the Popular Front government, which wanted the exhibition to serve as a tribute to socialism and radicalism, the unions refused to co-operate. Only certain foreign workers, such as the Belgians, the Russians and the Germans, working on their respective pavilions, kept to the timetable. It became obvious to the most casual bystander that very little would be achieved by the inauguration date. 'The Eiffel Tower is ready' was the standard joke of the time, and the opening was deferred. When President Lebrun, who had succeeded the assassinated Doumer in 1932, declared the exhibition open on 24 May 1937, very little was in place and the official cortège had to be carefully escorted around the buildings which had received a hurried cosmetic treatment to hide their rough edges. Once the President had left, work started up again and by the summer many hundreds of thousands of Parisians, people from the provinces and foreign tourists had enthusiastically viewed the Expo.

The King and Queen of England visited France from 19 to 22 July 1938. Although this might have been considered as simply another royal visit (King Carol of Roumania had attended the 14 July celebrations in 1937), the enthusiasm and warmth with which Paris greeted the British sovereigns was exceptional. The city was filled with posters asking Parisians to decorate their buildings and to display the colours of the two nations. 'Paris, interprète de la France', it was said, expressed its fidelity to the Franco-British alliance.

November 11, 1938, marked the twentieth anniversary of the Armistice. From every department in France torches were lit and carried to the tomb of the Unknown Soldier, so that the commemoration was spectacularly grandiose. Everywhere in France there were parades, speeches, soundings of the Last Post, two-minute silences and collective sadnesses.

July 1939 was also the 150th anniversary of the French Revolution, which supposedly had begun on 14 July 1789. Books, plays and films were commissioned, and on 12 July, on the initiative of the Paris authorities, the biggest flag in the world was unfurled at the Place de l'Hôtel de Ville, a *tricouleur* of 300 square metres. Five thousand children dressed in white drew out red and blue handkerchiefs to produce another *tricouleur*.

To all these festivities there was a sinister side. The International Exhibition had shown up labour troubles and had revealed a profound division within France. It was said that if you stood on the site and looked eastward you would see the popular *quartiers* of the Nation, Bastille, Saint-Antoine, profoundly hostile to the status quo, while to the west lay the *beaux quartiers*, resentful of the gains which socialism had made. The enthusiasm for the British royal family was an indication of the fear engendered by the Berlin-Rome axis. One commemoration of those who had died in 1918 posed the question of whether or not those deaths had served any purpose. The celebration of the 1789 Revolution provoked discussion as to whether the beginning of France's ills might not date from that event.

Through Paris, France tried to comfort herself. There was art, literature, culture and history. But the comfort was always uneasy. There was too much that was in the past and too little that was in the present. The present seemed to be dominated by the films of Fernandel, a comic actor who represented to perfection all the caricatural aspects of the French, and by the soft and caressing voice of Tino Rossi. After France had signed the Munich agreement, abandoned her alliance with Czechoslavakia and given way to Germany, Henri de Montherlant wrote, 'Over the half-dead corpse of a betrayed nation, France has surrendered to card-games and to Tino Rossi.'

ACHIEVEMENTS IN SPORT

Between the Wars sport made its mark in France. Hundreds of thousands of adults who had never played football in their lives became devoted spectators of the game, and in the south a passion for rugby developed. Cycling had always been a popular competitive sport all over France, particularly in the big cities, and, until increasing traffic made them impossible, bicycle races would take place in the suburbs. But the Tour de France was the sporting occasion of the year, a race which came directly to the people in their own villages. It was often said that for the old and infirm the greatest moment in their lives was the day on which the Tour went by.

Above left, Carpentier was the hero of the French boxing world. Simone de Beauvoir recalls that when he was knocked out by Jack Dempsey in 1921, Parisians wept in the streets. This photograph shows the Carpentier/Beckett fight of 1919.

Above right, Jules Ladoumègue, who broke the world 1500 metres record in 1930. A man of humble origins, he was denied a place in the 1932 Olympics because he had accepted payment and so lost his amateur status.

Right, The Olympic Games of 1924 at the height of French sporting achievement. Poster by Jean Droit.

Opposite, above At Le Mans.

Opposite, below, The start of the Six Jours, one of the most popular track races, in 1925.

PARIS_1924

JEUX OLYMPIQUES

There were several French directors who achieved worldwide fame in the 1930s and whose works are now regarded as classics of the cinema. René Clair made a series of notable films including *A Nous la liberté,* an obvious inspiration for Chaplin's *Modern Times,* with its satire of modern production methods and the amassing of wealth. Jean Renoir adapted many literary classics for the cinema, including Zola's harrowing novel *La Bête humaine,* in which heredity and destiny determine the tragic outcome. Marcel Pagnol was adept at reworking plays for the screen, using actors from southern France such as Raimu and Fernandel.

Marcel Carné usually worked in conjunction with the talented screenwriter, Jacques Prévert, and together they made the romantic fatalist film *Le Quai des brumes* (1938) with Jean Gabin, Michel Simon and Michèle Morgan, and the sombre *Le Jour se lève* (1939) about a working man caught up in violence and tragedy.

Carné focused on everyday life in the industrial suburbs and at the factory gates, and his point of view was generally pessimistic.

Above, A Nous la liberté (1931), directed by René Clair.

Below, La Bête humaine (1938), by Jean Renoir, starring Jean Gabin, Simone Simon and Bernard Blier.

Right, Marcel Pagnol's *Angèle* (1934), with the actor Fernandel.

Below, Le Roman d'un tricheur (1936), by Sacha Guitry, in which Guitry appeared in many disguises.

Above, Poster advertising Marcel Carné's film *Le Quai des brumes* (1938).

Below, Le Jour se lève (1939), by Carné, with Gabin and Arletty.

THE LITERARY ESTABLISHMENT

The Académie Française remained the centre of traditional literature. To be elected one of the 'immortals' was considered the greatest of honours; competition was always intense and often bitter. But the members of the Académie were not always France's most distinguished literary figures. The painting opposite, completed in 1935, includes men who were not normally thought of as writers.

Georges Duhamel was a representative writer of the period, the author of innumerable novels, essays and plays and the official representative of France in many international gatherings of writers.

Max Jacob was a Cubist poet and artist who converted from Judaism to Catholicism. A subtle and ironical writer, he was to die in a German concentration camp.

Paul Claudel wrote poetry and plays which embodied a mystical and sensuous Catholicism.

Alain (Emile-Auguste Chartier), philosopher and radical, was perhaps the most influential thinker of the interwar years. His newspaper essays, which counselled moderate and prudent living, tended towards a doctrine of self-interest.

Georges Duhamel, drawing by Serge Czerelkow (1927).

Max Jacob, self-portrait (1930).

Paul Claudel by Raoul Dufy (1921).

Alain. Photograph (1928).

Louis-Ferdinand Céline was the most vigorously polemical of the French writers of the period. His novels and pamphlets of the 1930s expressed a violent hatred of Jews, of the Soviet Union and of the condition of France, and prophesied a catastrophic war.

Léon Daudet (below) was a right-wing political journalist who, as Sennep shows, attacked traditional educational methods which encouraged belief in progress and in the Republic.

Cover of Céline's *Bagatelles pour un massacre* (1937).

Drawing by Matisse for a book by Henri de Montherlant (1937).

1 Picard   2 Prévost   3 Pétain   4 Valéry   5 Bergson   6 Mâle   7 Mauriac

In *La Trahison des clercs* (below), an influential work first published in 1927, Julien Benda expressed the view that French intellectuals should be guided by rational and abstract principles, and revealed his profound misgivings that this might no longer be the case.

Below, Louis Aragon, André Malraux and André Gide pay homage to Heinrich Mann, a refugee from Nazi Germany, 1936.

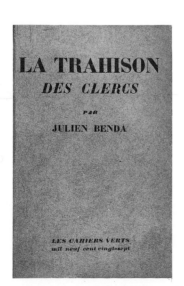

LA TRAHISON
DES CLERCS
PAR
JULIEN BENDA

LES CAHIERS VERTS
mil neuf cent vingt-sept

Mann   Aragon   Gide   Malraux

PARFUM **isabey**

THE **BEAUTY WORLD**

Beauty became a thriving business and the giants of cosmetics – Elizabeth Arden, Helena Rubinstein and Eugène Rimmel – conquered the Parisian market. Salons proliferated, offering a range of beauty treatments and products.

Colette opened her own salon in 1932, at the suggestion of André Maginot (after whom the Maginot line was named) and with the financial backing of the Pasha of Marrakesh and the Princesse de Polignac. She sold a line of cosmetics under her own name, but was less successful in the art of make-up than in the art of writing, and in 1933 she returned to her 'premier métier'.

Left, Poster advertising perfume, by Foujita, 1928.

Below, Advertisement for Simon cosmetics, 1929.

Ce n'est qu'un massage, Madame...
fait par le Moteur de Santé
SAVAGE

Trois modèles
en vente partout

Agents exclusifs :
ETOILE-IMPORTATION
78, Av^{nue} des Champs-Élysées, Paris

Ô femme
triste
esclave...

...que de soins
compliqués tu
consacres à ta
beauté, quand tu
pourrais, en cinq
minutes, par
l'usage conjugué
de la Crème, de
la Poudre et du
Savon Simon,
réaliser une
beauté saine qui
se prolonge du-
rant toute la vie!

CRÈME SIMON
·PARIS·

18,A   Pub. Wallace-Paris

Left, Advertisement for a slimming machine, 1929.

Opposite, Colette in her very modern beauty salon, in the rue de Miromesnil.

Êtes-vous pour, ou contre
le "second métier" de l'écrivain?

Colette

7, rue de
Miromesnil

119

VIEUX COLOMBIER

The Théâtre des Boulevards was a term referring to theatres which produced commercial plays for light entertainment, often using star actors. Marcel Pagnol's *Topaze* was a major success in 1928 and Sacha Guitry wrote more than a hundred plays, which he also produced and acted in.

Left, Copeau in Molière's *Les Fourberies de Scapin* at the Vieux Colombier.

Below, Berthe Bovy in Cocteau's *La Voix humaine* at the Comédie-Française.

Opposite
Top left, Poster for *La Vagabonde* (1923), an adaptation of Colette's novel.

Top centre, Poster for Sacha Guitry's *Un Tour au paradis.*

Top right, Poster for *Topaze* by Pagnol.

Bottom left, Jean Giraudoux and Louis Jouvet (*c.* 1930).

Bottom right, Poster for the first production of Giraudoux's *La Guerre de Troie n'aura pas lieu*, 1935.

THEATRE

The innovators in the theatre were strongly influenced by actor and director Jacques Copeau at the Vieux Colombier. Copeau rejected realism, favoured stylized stage movement, and preferred minimal scenery. The Cartel des Quatre, directed by Georges Pitoëff, Charles Dullin, Louis Jouvet and Gaston Baty, joined Copeau in his opposition to the academic style of the Comédie-Française and to commercial theatre. Jouvet collaborated with Jean Giraudoux, and from 1928 to 1940 he staged a new Giraudoux play almost every year, including in 1935 Giraudoux's masterpiece on the inevitability of war, *La Guerre de Troie n'aura pas lieu.*

In 1936 the satirical playwright Edouard Bourdet became administrator of the Comédie-Française and invited the Cartel directors to produce for him. Cocteau's *La Voix humaine* was an obvious sign of innovation, consisting of a single actress (Berthe Bovy) making a phone call to an invisible protagonist.

Berthe BOVY de la Comédie française dans la VOIE HUMAINE

RENAISSANCE
Ce soir, à 8 h. 1/2, PREMIÈRE
LA VAGABONDE
de Mme COLETTE et M. L. MARCHAND
avec
CORA LAPARCERIE
et
HARRY BAUR
Demain, MATINEE

MICHODIÈRE
Métro OPÉRA — 4 bis, Rue de la Michodière — Matinées 14 h 45 · Soirées 21 heures

VICTOR BOUCHER
HUGUETTE DUFLOS
et
JEAN PERIER
UN TOUR au PARADIS
Comédie en 4 Actes de M. SACHA GUITRY

BONVALLET   CHRISTIAN-GERARD
FORGET   Maud YREM   HELVET
G. PAYEN   Gaby BERGER   TAILLADE

Le RENARD et la GRENOUILLE
Comédie en 1 Acte de M. SACHA GUITRY

JEAN PERIER
GERMAINE RISSE
Katie VARLEY

MATINÉES : Dimanches et Fêtes

ATHÉNÉE
THÉATRE LOUIS JOUVET
4, SQUARE DE L'OPÉRA (RUE BOUDREAU) — LOCATION : OPÉRA 82-23

LA GUERRE DE TROIE
N'AURA PAS LIEU
PIÈCE EN 2 ACTES

DE JEAN GIRAUDOUX

LOUIS JOUVET	FALCONETTI
PIERRE RENOIR	MADELEINE OZERAY
ROMAIN BOUQUET	PAULE ANDRAL
JOSÉ NOGUERO	MARIE-HELENE DASTE
ROBERT BOGAR	ANNIE CARIEL
ANDRE MOREAU	ANDREE SERVILANGES
PIERRE MORIN	LISBETH CLAIRVAL
MAURICE CASTEL	ODETTE STUART
JULIEN BARROT	JACQUELINE MORANE
YVES GLADINES	GILBERTE GENIAT
ALFRED ADAM	VERA PHARES
JACQUES TERRY	PAUL MENAGER
BERNARD LANCREY	JEAN PERRIN
HENRI LIBERÉ	HENRI SAINT-ISLES

Musique de MAURICE JAUBERT

TOUS les SOIRS à 20 h. 45 · MATINEE DIMANCHES et FETES à 14 h. 45

MUSIC

Franco-German rivalry and hostility made itself felt even in the world of music. The French resented the easy assumption that the only real music was German music, and young composers after 1914 turned to Debussy, Fauré and Ravel as their masters. Cocteau, who appointed himself the artistic godfather of these musicians, was dissatisfied even with this. Debussy, he thought, was not only insufficiently French but had been influenced by the Russians, while Stravinsky echoed Wagner. Cocteau wanted French music to be true to itself and he recommended the eccentric Erik Satie (born in 1866), who lived in isolation at Arcueil. Satie's music was subtle, ironical and fragile and was considered very French.

The most experimental and adventurous music came from a group of young composers, initially called 'Les Nouveaux Jeunes', who came to be known as 'Les Six'. Their concerted efforts included *Album des Six* (1920) and *Les Mariés de la Tour Eiffel* (1921). Milhaud, one of their members, wrote

Left, Picasso's cover for the 1st edition (1919) of Stravinsky's piano arrangement of *Rag-time*.

Below left, Maurice Ravel, who died in 1937.

Below, Stravinsky at the piano in 1934, when he formally became a French citizen.

Opposite
Above: left and centre, Self-portrait by Erik Satie, 1919; writings by Satie.

Far right, Illustration for *Le Boeuf sur le toit*.

Below right, Cocteau sits in front of five of 'Les Six': Francis Poulenc, Germaine Tailleferre, Louis Durey, Darius Milhaud and Arthur Honegger. Behind them is Cocteau's portrait of the sixth, Georges Aurie.

Below left, The Swiss-born Honegger who, unlike the other members of 'Les Six', was interested in German music.

the music for *Le Boeuf sur le toit*, a music-hall spectacle, which was later made into a ballet. Cocteau organized the production and wrote the libretto; it was paid for by Etienne de Beaumont; and Dufy designed the scenery. First performed in February 1920, the production achieved great success, even when transferred to London.

UN GRAND MUSICIEN RUSSE SE FAIT NATURALISER FRANÇAIS. — Le célèbre compositeur Stravinsky, l'auteur de l' « Oiseau de Feu » et de « Petrouchka », qui réside en France depuis de nombreuses années, vient d'opter en faveur de sa patrie adoptive...

M. SADI

1 1 2

5,000,000 d'habitants!
TAUC de Sorciere:
PLUTONIE:
Nouvelle & vaste Contrée
de l'AFRIQUE centrale.
Les Nègres les plus noirs
du Monde.

LE BŒUF SUR LE TOIT
✤✤✤

La dame décolletée, le barman, le monsieur en habit, le nègre qui joue au billard, etc... dans un décor de Dufy et sur la musique de Darius Milhaud les personnages imaginés par Jean Cocteau se meuvent avec la lenteur des scaphandriers au fond de la mer — et accomplissent les gestes essentiels de leur vie. Tentative la plus intéressante qui soit. Cocteau rompt avec l'arbitraire glacé de la vie transportée au théâtre. Il en donne la synthèse, appliquée avec la plus vive intelligence au sens même de la réalisation scénique. ◊

Georges Auric

FASHION

Fashions changed. Women were looking for clothes that would reflect their more independent and relaxed lifestyle and would allow them greater freedom of movement. Paul Poiret failed to adapt his designs and ceased to appeal. The couturier who best responded to these new needs, with an extensive use of jersey and other knitted materials, was Coco Chanel. Chanel favoured shorter skirts, neat blouses, simple and elegant jackets, sweaters, cardigans and suits, and also pioneered the 'little black dress'. She carried her casual unfussy look even into her designs for evening gowns. Chanel also started the vogue for inexpensive costume jewellery. She was the first couturier whose expressed aim was to make fashion available to a wide range of women: 'Que ma mode descende dans la rue.'

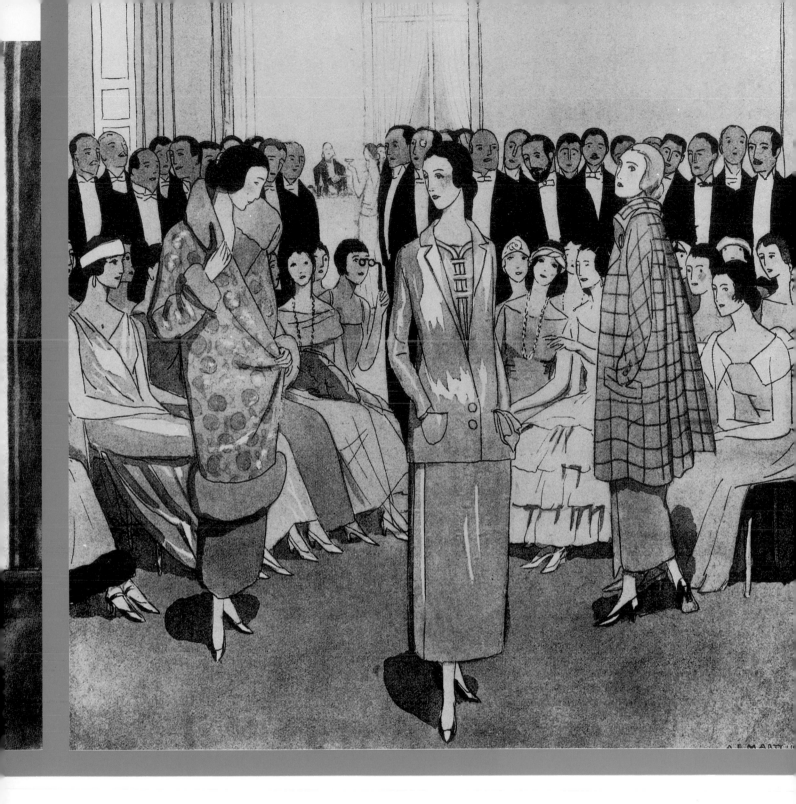

Jean Patou respected Chanel's taste, and he, too, designed with the modern sporty woman in mind. He was the first couturier to present previews for the press, an innovation soon adopted by other established houses, such as Doeuillet. In 1929 Patou showed a return to a more feminine line, with longer skirts, waisted dresses, and a predominance of curve over the straight line.

Left, Coco Chanel, who said 'Each frill discarded makes one look younger', in an evening gown which displays simplicity and elegance of line, worn with the ubiquitous pearls.

Centre, A striking coat design by Paul Poiret, 1923.

Right, Fashion show by Doeuillet in 1923.

EXPOSITION

PAR

ERNATIONALE
937

EXPOS OF ILLUSIONS

Preceding pages, The pavilions of Nazi Germany, on the left, and of the USSR face each other. The style of the art they represent is not dissimilar.

In 1937, Paris hosted another international exposition, devoted to technical achievements. Two of the most successful buildings were the Palais de l'Air and the Palais de la Lumière. The immense Palais de l'Air was a celebration of the progress made in aeronautics. It enclosed vast spaces bordered by painted blue skies and luminous clouds, where contemporary and futuristic aeroplanes simulated flight.

The most striking feature of Mallet-Stevens's Palais de la Lumière was a fresco by Raoul Dufy, dedicated to La Fée Electricité, which illustrated the history of electricity and the way in which it was transforming people's lives.

Below, Electrical generators in front of Dufy's La Fée Electricité.

Opposite, An aeroplane in full flight in the Palais de l'Air. All the machines were off the ground except for the plane which was used for training. In the background are paintings by Robert Delaunay.

THE **NORMANDIE**

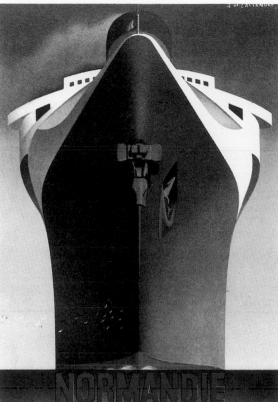

NORMANDIE
Cⁱᵉ Gᵉ TRANSATLANTIQUE
French Line
LE HAVRE – SOUTHAMPTON – NEW-YORK

The transatlantic liner *Normandie* was launched in 1932. Its lavish decor – the collective enterprise of some of the period's most representative architects, painters, sculptors and cabinet-makers – made it a dazzling showcase for French decorative arts.

It was also the grandest floating hotel of its time, complete with theatre, cinema, swimming pool, tennis courts, fashion shows and delectable cuisine. First-class passengers on the *Normandie*'s maiden voyage in 1935 included Jeanne Lanvin, Philippe Soupault, Paul Iribe and Colette. Later voyages had on board many emigrant families travelling 3rd class, making up one quarter of the 2000 passengers.

During the war, the *Normandie*, in port in New York, was destroyed by fire. With it sank Dunand's priceless lacquered panels and other masterpieces by Ruhlmann, Leleu, Süe, Dupas and Prou.

Opposite, The Grand Salon, and a third-class cabin designed by Mallet-Stevens (1935).

Above, Poster by Cassandre.

Left, The launching of the *Normandie* at Saint-Nazaire by Madame Lebrun, wife of the President of the Republic.

THE **FRENCH EMPIRE**

There were always Frenchmen who believed that not enough attention was paid to their empire. The French empire was considerable, including the North African territories of Morocco, Algeria and Tunisia (with some one-and-a-half million French inhabitants); the vast area of French West and French Equatorial Africa; Madagascar; French Indo-China; the French West Indies and the Pacific dependencies. School textbooks taught that French colonization was successful, and the writings of Gide, Montherlant and Duhamel, among others, stressed the exoticism of the overseas territories. Many films were set in the French colonies. There were, however, many who believed that colonialism led inevitably to corruption and injustice, and that it distracted France from her essential role in Europe. It was to counter such uncomfortable ideas that a great Colonial Exhibition was organized in 1931. As France became weaker, it was essential that France's greatness as an empire and the importance of its culture throughout the world be demonstrated.

Right, An advertisement for clothes suitable for wear in the colonies.

UNIFORMES et VÊTEMENTS pour les COLONIES
VÊTEMENTS PRÊTS A PORTER ET SUR MESURE
pour HOMMES, DAMES, JEUNES GENS, FILLETTES et ENFANTS

DJEBEL SAGHO

— La soumission, c'est encore rien... mais tu vas voir... la mission...

Far left, General Gouraud proclaiming the state of Greater Lebanon in July 1920. By arrangements made during the war, Syria and Lebanon became French mandates. Anonymous contemporary painting.

Above, At the Colonial Exhibition of 1931 full-scale replicas were built of several ancient monuments. The photograph shows the temple of Angkor-Vat in Cambodia.

Right, Because of the strong anti-clerical tradition in France there was often hostility to or mockery of missionary activities in the colonies. From Henri Barbusse's weekly, *Monde.*

THE
ROLE OF
RELIGION

Officially France was a Catholic country with small Protestant and Jewish minorities. The war encouraged the return to the Church of the middle classes, and by the 1920s the Church seemed to have weathered the crisis of positivism and modernism. There was an emphasis on public ceremony and an ostentatious enthusiasm for pilgrimages. It was in this period that the Church became politically involved in anti-Socialist and patriotic mass organizations which sometimes had Fascist undertones. In this period, too, sociological research revealed that a great many people in France had no religion at all and that for them Catholicism was merely a form of social conformism.

Opposite
Left, The ceremony of first commun-
ion is held in the devastated department of the Somme, in northern
France, 1919.

Below, Pilgrims in front of the grotto of
Lourdes, 1927.

On this page
Below, General de Castelnau, former
associate of Joffre and commander in
Alsace, was the leader of the Ligue
Catholique and of other Catholic organizations which believed that the
Church should play a more active part
in day-to-day politics. In this photograph he is addressing a crowd of
some 50,000 at Angers, using the newly
developed microphone (1925).

Right, Perret was the architect of this
church at Le Raincy, one of Paris's
growing suburbs (1922-23).

ART AS ENCHANTMENT

By the 1930s the great painters who had made Paris the centre of the art world were no longer young. Even Cubism and Fauvism belonged to the past. Expressionism and Surrealism now placed the emphasis not on abstract values (form, line, colour) but on emotion and content. Matisse came to stand outside all these movements. His later paintings go farther than those of any of his contemporaries towards decorative beauty and pure pleasure in the physical world. In his *Pink Nude*, 1935 (right), an impression of volume and sensuousness is achieved by the simplest of means – the result, however, of twenty-two preliminary studies. Working in sculpture, such as the bronze *Reclining Woman*, 1929 (right, below), helped him to master three-dimensional form.

Derain, too, turned to a more sensuous inspiration in his maturity. This woodcut of a nude holding a flower (below) is an illustration to Apollinaire's *L'Enchanteur pourrissant*, 1921.

ART
AS SCULPTURE

Right, Jean Arp came to Paris in 1922. This bronze torso (1931) reflects the rounded forms of his style after 1930, when he abandoned geometrical shapes.

Below, Brancusi was steeped in the popular traditions of his native Romania. His shapes became increasingly simple and more and more evocative. One of his favourite subjects was Mademoiselle Pogany, whom he represented as a stylized head with bulging eyes and a long sinuous neck. He made many variations of this sculpture, most of them in marble or polished bronze. This brass version dates from 1920.

Below right, Laurens' bronze, *Woman Bathing* (1931), reveals the influence of Cubism, as well as conveying a sense of movement.

Opposite, Picasso's interest in sculpture was revived in 1928. He produced mostly welded iron constructions, but there were exceptions, such as this magnificent cockerel in bronze (1932).

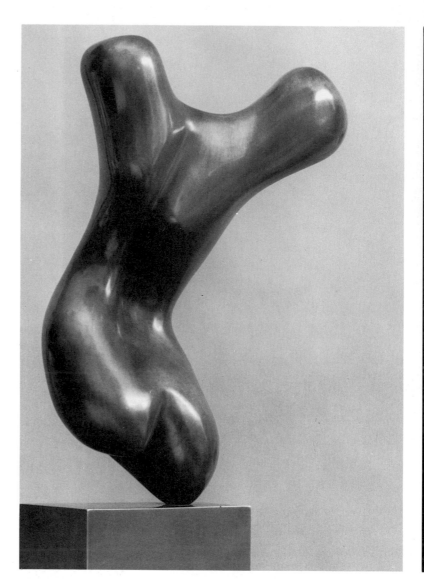

The Maginot Line, built by the French between the wars.

The French Institute of Public Opinion was created in 1938. Through it we know that in August 1938, 78 percent of French men (women were not polled) thought that the *entente* between France and Britain would succeed in maintaining peace in Europe. In April 1939, 47 percent thought that the year 1939 would end without a war, and in July 1939, only 45 percent, still a minority, believed that there would be a war. Thus within a few weeks of the outbreak of war in 1939, there was no overwhelming sense of its inevitability.

Doubtless the experience of Munich in September 1938 had something to do with it. On 23 and 24 September the French mobilized more than a million civilians. As in 1914, notices were posted outside the *mairies*; railway stations became the settings of many painful partings. But then there was the meeting at Munich, where the French Prime Minister – once again Daladier (since April 1938) – together with Neville Chamberlain, Hitler and Mussolini, abandoned France's ally Czechoslovakia and made peace. In October, an opinion poll showed that 37 percent of those who were interviewed disapproved of the Munich agreement (as did Daladier himself).

The truth is that the nation was as uncertain and divided as was its government. There were those who were confident: Hitler was bluffing, Germany could not withstand a long war because of her economic weakness, the French army (as was demonstrated each successive 14 July) was the finest in the world, France had a magnificent Empire, and Britain (with the Commonwealth) was a redoubtable ally. But there were those who could not bring themselves to contemplate another devastating war like that of 1914, who believed that the nation was far from united and who feared that a war would bring about a Communist revolution, who were apprehensive about Germany's air-strength, who thought that some sort of an agreement with Germany was possible. These divisions surfaced in 1939, when the Foreign Minister, Georges Bonnet, tried to pretend that the German invasion of Poland on 1 September had not taken place and tried to find another Munich-type agreement through the intervention of Italy. But Daladier declared that Hitler's signature no longer had any value. The same divisions became even clearer after 10 May 1940, when the German armies began their triumphant offensive in Holland, Belgium and France. Marshal Pétain became the leader of those who wanted peace and an agreement with Hitler (while there were some who sought a more active co-operation with the Germans); General de Gaulle, in London, became the symbolic leader of those who wished the struggle to continue (while within France resistance movements became more organized).

The reasons for defeat must begin by a consideration of the military errors: a belief in static warfare which would be dominated by the Maginot Line; a constant over-planning which meant that the army was unable to improvise; a misunderstanding of the German plan of attack. But although these were important, no one believes that they alone caused the disaster which went well beyond military defeat and led to the downfall of the Republic. The fact that the government was divided into pro-armistice and anti-armistice groups was important. It was alleged that the defeat had occurred and the Republic had foundered because the politicians and an inefficient political system had failed to prepare France adequately for the ordeal of war. It was claimed that certain sections of the bourgeoisie preferred to have an agreement with the Germans rather than run the risk of a return to the Popular Front, and the remark of an obscure journalist, 'Better Hitler than Léon Blum', was regarded as though it were a widely held belief.

Two things stand out. One, that the Popular Front government from 1936 to 1937 did make the French increasingly class-conscious and did heighten social tensions; the other, that it was in these years that the need for national unity was most acutely felt. It was impossible for Blum, or for any of his successors, to reconcile these antagonistic strands of French history.

France has never forgotten the days of defeat and humiliation, and the history of Vichy, of the Resistance and of Gaullism are still subjects of controversy and bitterness. But all these elements of French history resembled each other in so far as they all wanted a new France. Such a France did not emerge automatically at the Liberation. But the experience of the years of illusion played its part in the slow process of forging a creative and independent France with a new sense of nationhood.

THE END OF THE POPULAR FRONT

When Léon Blum's Popular Front government resigned in 1937, the government which succeeded, headed by Camille Chautemps, showed that the Radicals had now taken the lead. The alliance which made up the Popular Front became increasingly difficult to maintain. The Communists pushed for a revival of the Front, but without success. In January 1938 Blum tried to form a coalition which would construct a national government going beyond the dimensions of the Popular Front, from the Communist leader Thorez to the right-centre Independent Reynaud. But he failed, and when he did return to power in March 1938, his government lasted only a few weeks, although it is notable for having sketched a more modern, and Keynesian, approach to the economic crisis. The government that succeeded, that of Daladier, contained several ministers who were adversaries of the Popular Front. Thus it was paradoxical that with the same Chamber of Deputies as had marked the triumph of the Popular Front in the elections of 1936, the government was of a totally different colour.

Right, Léon Blum emerges from a meeting with the President of the Republic, 4 April 1938. It was then obvious that his government would not last and it was defeated four days later.

Opposite
Above, On 25 and 26 September 1938, Premier Daladier came to London to confer with his British colleagues. On his right is Georges Bonnet, an appeaser, who was Foreign Minister; on his left the Commander in Chief, Gamelin, who was pessimistic about the possibilities of the Czech army resisting a German invasion.

Below left, King George and Queen Elizabeth leaving the Quai d'Orsay Palace to entertain the French President at the British Embassy, 20 July 1938.

Below right, La Grande Illusion continues.

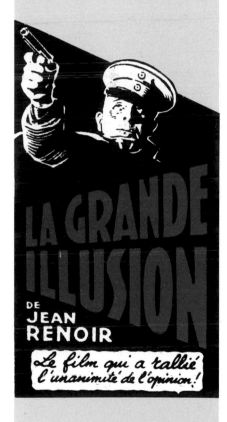

LA GRANDE ILLUSION DE JEAN RENOIR
Le film qui a rallié l'unanimité de l'opinion!

Top, The *Action Française* newspaper organizes opinion against the government of Edouard Herriot, who wanted France to honour her debts to America. He was defeated on this issue and resigned 14 December 1932.

Centre, The emblem of the Action Française, centred on the fleur de lys, the symbol of royalism.

Right, Marching song in praise of Mussolini, late 1920s. French nationalists were embarrassed by Italian claims to Nice, Corsica and Tunisia, but admired Mussolini for his energy and the discipline he was supposed to have instilled in Italy.

Opposite
Top left, The Croix-de-Feu as the supposed antidote to Communism, 1934.

Top right, Nationalists were not always in favour of foreign dictators. This 1935 cartoonist laments that the French governments have not kept Hitler out of the Saar.

Below, Croix-de-Feu parade down the Champs-Elysées in 1935. Though the Croix-de-Feu appeared to be the main movement of the right, in practice its leader, Colonel de la Rocque, was somewhat hesitant.

144

THE NATIONALIST RIGHT

It has been estimated that when Hitler came to power some 370,000 French people belonged to groups which could be termed Fascist. As is always the case in French politics, there was no unity among these Fascist groups and some were more radical or more romantic than others. All, however, were nationalist. The Action Française was the oldest, having been founded in 1898 to combat the anti-militarists and the supporters of Dreyfus. It was a royalist group, and presented the most coherent version of an alternative society – traditionalist, hierarchical, disciplined and allied to the Catholic Church. Alongside the Action Française was the Croix-de-Feu, an organization of ex-servicemen which grew rapidly in the 1930s to some 150,000 members.

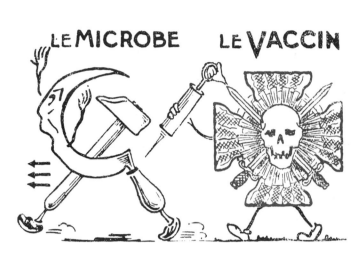

ANTI-WAR

Pacifist and anti-war feeling in France took many forms. Among Socialists in particular, there was the feeling that all men should be brothers, that war was only for the benefit of armament manufacturers, that all concessions were preferable to a situation where a single peasant would be killed. Among the nationalists on the right, there was the allegation that France was being manoeuvred (by the Jews, the Spanish Popular Front, the Communists) into involvement in conflicts which did not concern her. Everywhere, particularly in the countryside and in the small towns, there was a deep hatred and fear of all war.

— Merci... j'aime mieux : « Vivre pour la France ! »

CENTRE SYNDICAL D'ACTION CONTRE LA GUERRE

Correspond. : A. JUIN, 61, rue de l'Arcade, PARIS - 8e

ASSEZ!
BASTA! GENUG!
ДОВОЛЬНО! ENOUGH!
D04860

Opposite, above, Le Corbusier's cover design for the Pavillon des Temps Nouveaux in the 1937 International Exhibition calls for houses rather than arms.

Opposite, below, One of Braque's series of *Vanitas* still-lifes (1939). Although Braque claimed to eschew any symbolism in his work, the timing of these still-lifes and their overwhelming sense of mortality suggests that he was not unaffected by the threat of another war.

Left, A cartoon in the right-wing *Je Suis Partout* in 1938 shows a French soldier preferring to live for France, rather than die for other countries and causes.

Above, The workers of all countries reject war. Trade union poster of January 1939.

COUP DE THEATRE
après l'extrême tension :
Aujourd'hui à 15 heures, à Munich, conférence
CHAMBERLAIN-DALADIER-HITLER-MUSSOLINI

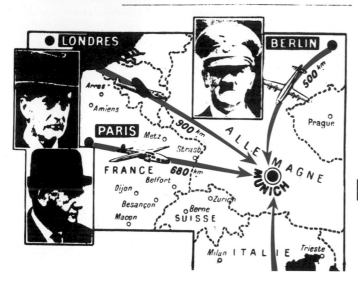

Sollicité par l'Angleterre M. Mussolini a demandé par téléphone au Führer de surseoir vingt-quatre heures à la mobilisation générale envisagée pour hier

LE CHANCELIER HITLER A ACCEPTÉ

MUNICH AND THE UPPER CLASSES

Like other nations, the French were moved by the drama of Hitler's last-minute decision to agree to hold a conference in Munich to avoid war in 1938. On 27 September conflict seemed imminent but the next day there appeared to be hope for peace. Not many believed, as one Socialist put it, that peace at any price was war at any price. Apart from the Communists who voted against, only Henri de Kerillis, the right-wing editor of the newspaper *L'Époque*, opposed the Munich agreements.

The upper classes continued their usual pursuits. In this context it is curious to note that *La Règle du jeu*, Renoir's film about social break-up and the mediocrity and falseness of French society, went into production shortly after Munich. Set in a luxurious château, the film follows the fortunes of both masters and servants to a tragic dénouement. Its protagonist, played by Renoir himself, claims that everyone in the world tells lies – governments, the radio, the cinema, the newspapers ... 'Why then', he asks, 'should we, ordinary individuals, not tell lies as well?'

Opposite, above, Announcement of the Munich conference on 29 September, 1938.

Opposite, below, Jean Renoir in *La Règle du jeu.* When the film was shown a few weeks before the outbreak of war it was a complete failure.

Above, It is ironical that one of the most popular songs just before the war told the story of a Marquise who telephones her butler, and who, little by little, verse by verse, learns of a series of disastrous events. But the butler always reassures her. 'Apart from that,' he says, 'tout va très bien, tout va très bien.'

Right, Elegant crowds watch the fireworks at Longchamp in 1939. The next 14 July would be very different.

GENERAL STRIKE

In 1937 and 1938 there had been a number of serious strikes (in the Goodrich tyre factory and in the Paris métro and bus services). In 1938 Paul Reynaud, Finance Minister in Daladier's government, convinced of the necessity for rearmament, sought to abolish one of the most cherished achievements of the Popular Front, the 40-hour week. This, and other measures including increases in taxation, were imposed by decree. The main trade union, the Confédération Générale du Travail, called a general strike in November 1938. It was a failure, and many strikers in government employ were dismissed. Even the workers were not united.

Far left, above, Workers at the Crespin steelworks in Valenciennes give the Communist salute, fly the red flag and display an effigy of Daladier.

Far left, below, The Communist newspaper, *L'Humanité,* calls for a general strike. Those in favour of such action wanted also to discredit the Daladier government which had signed the Munich agreement.

Left, The Crespin workers occupy the factory.

LA MODE S'ADAPTE AUX ÉVÉNEMENTS
« Bleu alerte » et capuchon « pour l'abri »
La générale Gamelin et Mme Jean Giraudoux présentes à la première « collection » 39-40

UNE PREMIÈRE PRÉSENTATION DE MODES DE GUERRE A PARIS

(Dessin de Réois Manvel)

THE **PHONEY WAR**

From September 1939 until the spring of 1940 nothing much seemed to happen. The conscripts were bored. They had nothing to do. The farmworkers wanted to get back to the land. Life seemed to be going on as usual.

Above, The first fashion show of the war took place almost as though nothing had changed but the titles of the designs, with their mention of air-raids. Such patriotic chic was typical of the phoney war.

Right, Two British soldiers from Guildford spend their leave in Paris. For them the war, so far, is unexpected tourism.

Opposite, The pride of the French defence system was the Maginot Line, begun in 1930. Inside this great technical achievement troops lived in a world of their own, keeping the long passages, with their railway tracks, neat and tidy.

Above, Mounted German troops ride down the Champs-Elysées at midday on Friday 14 June. Of the 5 million inhabitants of the Paris region, some 3 million had fled.

Opposite, 'L'Exode': French families flee.

Right, The cult of Marshal Pétain, here shown at the great victory parade of 14 July 1919, and later, in civilian clothes, assuring a French peasant that France will rise again. Popular prints.

DEFEAT

The German offensive began on 10 May. By 13 May the Wehrmacht had crossed the river Meuse and was heading westward towards the Channel ports. The French command attempted to establish a line of defence stretching from Abbeville to the Maginot Line, but by the second week of June the Germans had broken

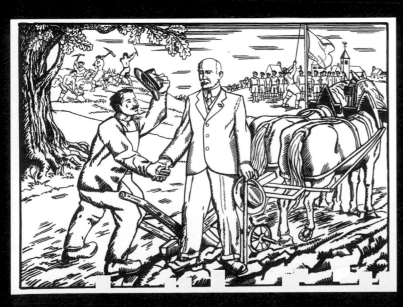

through. It was decided not to defend Paris, and early on the morning of 14 June German troops started to enter the capital.

One of the characteristics of the campaign was the panic which overtook the civilian populations. Remembering perhaps how ten French departments had been occupied by the Germans for four long years in the 1914 War, millions of people got on the roads and went south and westward. Small towns of a few hundred inhabitants found themselves 'invaded' by some 40,000, looking for somewhere to sleep and desperate for food. It looked as if the whole structure of French society might collapse. Paul Reynaud resigned as Premier on 16 June and Marshal Pétain declared in a broadcast speech the next day that the French would have to give up ('Il faut cesser le combat').

Immediately after Reynaud had resigned and Pétain had formed a government on 16 June, the new Foreign Minister, Pierre Baudouin, approached the Spanish Ambassador, asking him to arrange armistice talks with the Germans. Hitler, determined to redress history, insisted that these talks be held in Marshal Foch's old railway carriage at Rethondes, where General Huntziger was France's representative. The very fact that Pétain had assumed power was also a tribute to the past. The hero of Verdun was the most prestigious of Frenchmen because of his war record. The relatively unknown General de Gaulle, who had served for a few weeks as a junior minister, sought to break with the past. He arrived in London on 17 June to establish Free France. A general without an army, without money, without followers, de Gaulle nevertheless established himself as the leader of the French resistance, both from outside and from inside France. He pointed the way to Liberation and to the future.

Above, General Huntziger, handing the request for armistice to General Keitel in the 'Wagon de l'Armistice' at Rethondes on 22 June 1940.

Top, Marshal Pétain, aged 84, leader of those who wanted peace and an agreement with the Germans.

Opposite, De Gaulle in England.

SELECTIVE INDEX INCLUDING ILLUSTRATIONS AND CREDITS